THE CHRISTIAN CAPITALIST

THE GOSPEL OF HARD WORK AND GENEROUS GIVING

BY
RICH SANDERS

As for those who in the present age are rich, command them not to be haughty, or to set their hopes on the uncertainty of riches, but rather on God who richly provides us with everything for our enjoyment. They are to do good, to be rich in good works, generous, and ready to share, thus storing up for themselves the treasure of a good foundation for the future, so that they may take hold of the life that really is life.

—St. Paul's First Letter to Timothy (6:17–19)

CONTENTS

ACKNOWLEDGMENTS

I thank my wife, Rebekah, for listening to me talk about this project for three years and all of her outstanding editing work. Thanks to our children: James, Will, and Caroline; they have been very supportive throughout this process. Finally, I appreciate all the editorial assistance provided by Megan Atkinson, Kristen Gibbs, Martin Heintzelman, and Adriana Herrarte-Wirth.

INTRODUCTION

This book is a guide for Christians who are also capitalists at every level of the economy. While the Gospel addresses economic issues in numerous areas, we explore how Christianity and capitalism can work together in a very simple way: the more we make, the more we give!

While many Christians today recognize that it is important to work hard, what about the fruits of that labor? Especially as more Americans than ever identify as "spiritual but not religious," what is the new model for giving when a person doesn't go to church and thus has no interest in the old ways of tithing (or giving 10 percent to a church)?

Here is an anecdote from a conversation after a church service a few years ago that illustrates the concern:

"Rich, I need to talk with you after the service." As a young pastor, I was so excited to get this request! The member of the church was a young man who had already established himself in business, he had recently gotten married and was thinking about starting a family. When he asked to speak with me after the service, I wondered if it was going to be related to all these new family developments.

"What's on your mind?" I ask. "I just need to talk to you. It's about our financial goals." I thought, *That's really interesting!* This young professional guy was attending services regularly with his wife, but he had not made a significant contribution to the financially unstable church, despite my pleas to the congregation. I was hoping that he was getting ready to make a pledge to regularly donate to the church or maybe even talk about some kind of lump-sum gift. While we had not had any particular urgent needs arise, the church was struggling. We were regularly having budget meetings to look at cuts, and there were some capital improvements that had been delayed for years. A big contribution would really be helpful and timely.

After the service, he came to my office at the church and sat down. He closed the door behind him, which didn't surprise me, given that we were going to be talking about money. As he sat down, I asked him, "Well, I hope y'all are doing well." He said that they were and that that was one of the reasons he wanted to speak with me.

"Rich, I've given this a lot of thought, and I'd like to ask for your advice. We've been working very diligently on developing a home budget now that we've been married for a little over a year. I've decided that it's time to set some financial goals, and that's what I want to talk to you about."

"That's fantastic! Budgeting is a really important part of setting up a new home. It can help avoid conflict down the road when y'all face unexpected expenses. I'm delighted that you're taking this effort."

"Yep, and now that I've set my financial goals, I want to talk with you about this idea. One of my financial goals is . . . **I want to buy a Lamborghini!**"

I was stunned! I couldn't think of why on Earth this young man could talk about responsible budgeting and financial goal setting and then come to such a material conclusion. It's not like I had a Lamborghini dealership!

"What does that have to do with me?" I blurted out.

"Well," he replied, "you see, our church is out here in a rural area, and I know that you live in the city. I wonder if you know anybody who's got a Lamborghini who can point me in the right direction for a dealer."

Shaking my head, I said, "I'm sorry, friend, I think you've come to the wrong place. I wouldn't know a Lamborghini from a Ferrari, and I certainly don't know anyone who drives one or sells them. I wish I could be of more help!

"Just one more thing," I added. "Have you prayed during this budgeting and financial goal setting process?

"No, why?" he responded.

"Just something to think about. All we have comes from God, so you might want to think about how to give some back," I said.

He smiled. "I sure will."

That was so deflating! Walking into that meeting, I thought we were going to have a conversation about stewardship and how he could make an impact at the church with his newfound wealth, but it ended up being a conversation about an Italian race car! It felt like all my sermons about stewardship and remembering God as the source of all we have had been a waste of time.

I moved to a different church soon after that, so I'm not sure whatever happened with that young man's mission to get a Lamborghini. I'll tell you this, though, without remembering God in his development of a financial plan, he was building his house on sand.

I'm not going to criticize him for setting a tangible goal like buying a fancy Italian sports car. As a capitalist, it is fair to plan to acquire material things with the amounts we earn, especially with such an expensive, flamboyant purchase; however, the part that troubled me about our conversation is that he had missed the message altogether of sharing resources with the needy.

For Christian Capitalists, working hard is not only enjoyable but is also necessary. The accumulation of wealth is a natural result of hard work. When that accumulation gets to be significant enough that someone can afford more than $100,000 for a car, however, it should be accompanied by some reflection of God's blessing that allowed the person to be in a position to acquire those material goods in the first place.

As a Christian Capitalist, if you are ready to spend millions on a house, or $100,000 on a car, or take an expensive vacation around the world, you should be ready to give a significant amount to the poor. Every single thing we have is the result of God's blessing. That includes the drive to work hard, earn more, and give more.

This topic has a sense of urgency because various religious movements in the twenty-first century propose an agenda of socialism. The economic turmoil and resulting economic boom caused by COVID-19 may have changed American opinions on capitalism. In a September 2022 study by Pew Research Center, 36 percent of US adults said they view socialism somewhat or very positively, down from 42 percent who viewed the term positively in May 2019. Today, six in ten say they view socialism negatively, including one-third who view it very negatively.[1]

Furthermore, the Pew Research Center states that a majority of the public (57 percent) continues to view capitalism favorably. However, that is eight percentage points lower than in 2019 (65 percent).[2] Based on these recent data, it appears that public opinion of capitalism and socialism may fluctuate depending on the current economic landscape and may be subject to annual changes.

Although there's certainly a social and economic divide over the issue, the greater concern for Christian Capitalists is generational. Pew Research Center reports that younger adults have a more positive impression of socialism than their older counterparts. As socialism has gained popularity in recent years, fewer Americans than ever before identify as Christian. While 64 percent of Americans claim to be Christians today, the Pew Research Center stated in a September 2022 study that less than half of Americans will be Christians by 2070 if the declining trend continues.[3]

With this sense of urgency in mind, this book serves as a companion to Christians in both their giving and their work. Beyond the annual stewardship drive for a church or the call from a pastor to "give 'til it hurts," the particular purpose of this instruction is to motivate Christians to work hard and share the blessings of that work—the literal fruit of their labor—with the world in the name of Jesus Christ.

Many of the most devout Christians in America are wealthy. They intend to follow Christ's path and his instructions. However, when confronted with some of the parables of Jesus, which would compel a person to give away everything he or she has, they become concerned. Many of these goodhearted folks are not only wealthy, but they also have their fortune by counseling others on growing their fortunes! Financial advisors, stockbrokers, financial planners, and all other sorts of professionals who grow wealthy by helping others grow wealthy are often some of the most troubled Christians. One of the main purposes of this book is to confront these difficult teachings of Jesus and help these good Christians make sense of their lives.

This book is not just for financial professionals but for anyone who earns a living and becomes financially successful regardless of what that success looks like. Such individuals often struggle with Jesus's teachings about money and wealth. When some of these good people buy a house or a new car or send a child to a private school, they often struggle with a sense of guilt or discord with God. When they drive a new car, wear a new suit or dress to church, and hear some of the Gospel lessons that we address here, they cannot help but become concerned that they are living their lives off the path of Christ.

Jesus challenges us in the parables and in the lessons of the Gospel, and we cannot simply pay those lessons lip service. Instead, we must try to make sense of them in light of our American capitalist society. Time and time again, Holy Scripture tells us that people are rewarded for following God and trusting in Him. While this has led pastors over the last few decades to declare a Prosperity Gospel, which many Christians find popular, the fundamental premise of this book is that a Gospel of Hard Work and Generous Giving will lead to a closer relationship with God.

As Paul wrote in his first letter to the early Christians:

As for those who in the present age are rich, command them not to be haughty, or to set their hopes on the uncertainty of riches, but rather on God who richly provides us with everything for our enjoyment. They are to do good, to be rich in good works, generous, and ready to share, thus storing up for themselves the treasure of a good foundation for the future, so that they may take hold of the life that really is life. (1 Timothy 6:17–19)

This direction from Paul to Timothy about early Christians still rings true 2,000 years later! From a modern perspective, if a simple summary of the doctrine behind the Gospel of Hard Work and Generous Giving could be given, it is **the more we make, the more we give!**

As the number of Christians in the United States continues to decline, and likewise the number of people embracing socialism continues to increase over the long-term (possibly depending on the status of the economy), it is imperative that Christian Capitalists continue to not only earn and make their fortunes but also give generously to the poor and needy. After all, what fuels the anti-Christian movement is an increasingly popular sentiment that Christianity either holds no value or is populated by people who contradict the principles of Jesus in their everyday lives. Likewise, people promoting a socialist agenda in the United States advocate for it based on providing a greater benefit to all so that socioeconomic disparities become less extreme.

A Gospel of Hard Work and Generous Giving, however, can be a bridge for those two disparate philosophies. We should be walking in the path of Jesus toward a closer relationship with God by following the teachings of the Gospel and spreading the Good News to everyone in their daily work. Then, because making more money or maintaining a profitable venture is not an end unto itself, Christian Capitalists give generously from the profit that they have made. In this book, we will explore various scriptural references that support these twin pillars: working to make a productive benefit from talents and materials that God has provided us and giving generously to share those benefits with our neighbors in the name of Jesus Christ. As we progress through the Holy Scripture, we will analyze various passages that relate to these concepts of productivity and generosity to ultimately develop a philosophy that is uniquely Christian and capitalist!

PART I

WORKING AND GIVING AS CHILDREN OF GOD

CHAPTER 1

WE ARE MADE IN GOD'S IMAGE TO WORK

What do we know about God? In the very first verses of the Holy Bible, the book of Genesis tells us one thing about God: He works! In the course of creating the heavens and the Earth, the deep and the dryland, the day and the night, all the animals and the plants and the trees, and then finally humankind itself, the very first action we see our Lord take is work: "Then God said, 'Let us make humankind in our image, according to our likeness . . .' So God created humankind in [H]is image, in the image of God [H]e created them; male and female [H]e created them." (Genesis 1:26–27).[1] God took Adam and put him in the garden of Eden to till it and keep it (Genesis 2:15). The sole purpose of the first human was to work!

People are productive. They are meaningful, and they give life. Most of all, they have a purpose. Working for a purpose is God's way. On the seventh day, He rested after blessing and sanctifying this sabbath day because He had worked hard (Genesis 2:2–3). Instead of going on a permanent vacation or sitting back and admiring all the things He had done in the first six days, He went back to work after a day of rest.

As the stories of Scripture unfold to include Adam and Eve, Noah and the Ark, and Abraham and Sarah, we continue to find God at work in the universe and in the lives of those early humans. It is this notion, of working for a purpose, that is the foundation not just of all Christian work ethic but also of God's relationship with humans. After God leads the people of Israel out of slavery into freedom and the wilderness, Moses visits with his father-in-law, Jethro. As the priest of Midian, Jethro has experience in handling people and conflict, and he gives Moses some advice on how to balance his workload. He gives this further instruction: "Now listen to me. I will give you counsel, and God be with you! You should represent the people before God, and you should bring their cases before God; teach them the statutes and instructions and make known to them the way they are to go and the things they are to do" (Exodus 18:19–20). Even Jethro, Moses's father-in-law and a new convert to the ways of God, understands that people need to work as part of God's design for them.

Time and time again throughout history, we find examples of productive people—and, thus, productive societies—flourishing as those who are not productive and capable of evolving through work waste away on the vine of human history. God establishes the schedule of our daily lives in this manner. The Second Commandment is "Remember the sabbath day, and keep it holy. Six days you shall labor and do all your work. But the seventh day is a sabbath to the Lord your God; you shall not do any work . . ." (Exodus 20:8–10; also

Exodus 34:21). Work is hardwired into our nature with God because we are made in His image.

Furthermore, even as we are made in His image, this human work ethic derives from our desire to follow the path that God sets for us in creation. It is His desire for us, but it is uniquely our path to follow. From our earliest days, we set about work, recognizing that this was God's design for us and is ours to embrace. As Moses followed God's instructions in constructing the Holy of Holies and the Ark of the Covenant, the people of Israel, men and women alike, "All the Israelite men and women whose hearts made them willing to bring anything for the work that the Lord had commanded by Moses to be done, brought it as a free will offering to the Lord" (Exodus 35:29; also Exodus 36:1–10). They brought so much that Moses had to tell them to stop!

It follows, therefore, that our desire for work is as innate as our desire to work hard. It is this desire to work hard that fuels capitalism, especially the uniquely American form, and that, in many ways, helped build the nation that we enjoy today.

WE WORK TO BE CLOSER TO GOD

The reasons we work are fairly basic at their roots. We work to survive, and we work to help others survive.

This notion of working for a purpose is so important that modern Christians have started referring to it as a calling. We pray, reflect, and try to find work that feels as though we are accomplishing God's will. Many Christians, however, have fallen into the habit of using this word to only describe work in ministry. This is simply too narrow an understanding of the importance of work in our lives and our makeup.

God made us in His own image. Because the very first thing we know about Him is that He works, our image in the likeness of God thus includes an innate ability and desire to work. This is especially true of the people of Israel in Egypt. As Pharaoh held them captive and made them work only for his interests, God sent Moses to lead the people to freedom. God flipped the narrative for His people, as we would say in modern times. He worked for them by saving them from slavery in Egypt. Then, "Israel saw the great work that the Lord did against the Egyptians. So the people feared the Lord and believed in the Lord and in his servant Moses" (Exodus 14:31).

God's work is perfect. His work includes all of creation, including us! It is our whole duty as humans, not just as Christian Capitalists, to work and follow His commandments. Going back to the story of Noah and the Ark, we know from ancient times that God sees our work. When He accepts it, we have reason to rejoice! "Go, eat your bread with enjoyment, and drink your wine with a merry heart; for God has long ago approved what you do" (Ecclesiastes 9:7). This provides an incentive for us to work hard during our lives and put everything we have into our work: "Whatever your hand finds to do, do with your might . . ." (Ecclesiastes 9:10). Once we are done, God ". . . will bring every deed into judgment, including every secret thing, whether good or evil" (Ecclesiastes 12:14). With these ancient Hebrew Scriptures in place, the foundation of the work ethic of the modern Christian Capitalist is established.

WE WORK TO BUILD COMMUNITY WITH OTHERS

The tension with capitalism has always been straightforward: How can a person strive to maximize production, and thus wealth, while still loving his neighbor? The proponents of socialism, particularly those who contend that socialism is the economic model that fits most closely with Christian doctrine, point to this tension as the primary reason capitalism and Christianity are at odds. Simply put, socialists argue that capitalism requires greed and the exploitation of others to function.

The hard work that fuels capitalism, however, is ingrained in all humans from our earliest days. Furthermore, this desire for hard work does not put us at odds with others; instead, it pushes us to work together. After God led the people out of slavery in Egypt into the wilderness and on the way to the promised land, Moses directed the people to build a sanctuary to God.

Bezalel and Oholiab and every skillful one to whom the Lord has given skill and understanding to know how to do any work in the construction of the sanctuary shall work in accordance with all that the Lord has commanded.

Moses then called Bezalel and Oholiab and every skillful one to whom the Lord had given skill, everyone whose heart was stirred to come to do the work; and they received from Moses all the freewill offerings that the Israelites had brought for doing the work on the sanctuary. They still kept bringing him freewill offerings every morning, so that all the artisans who were doing every sort of task on the sanctuary came, each from the task being performed, and said to Moses, "The people are bringing much more than enough for doing the work that the Lord has commanded us to do."

So Moses gave command, and word was proclaimed throughout the camp: "No man or woman is to make anything else as an offering for the sanctuary." So the

people were restrained from bringing; for what they had
already brought was more than enough to do all the
work. (Exodus 36:1–8)

The people of Israel not only worked hard to build the sanctuary, but they gave also so much of their own accord that Moses
had to tell them to stop giving!

Once we provide for ourselves, we provide for our families. Once we provide for our families, however, that's where
things get interesting. The accumulation of property and currency savings beyond what we need is frequently described as
wealth. What then, does the Christian Capitalist do with the
wealth he or she has accumulated? Scripture has another basis
for wealth: working for our own survival innately includes
working to help others. That's how God made us.

Holy Scripture paints a picture of working to achieve
God's will for us, and that work has a direct impact on the
community. The way to "love your neighbor as yourself" is
through our work. Although Jesus reiterated "love your neighbor as yourself" as the great Second Commandment later in
the Gospels, this concept is as old as the people of Israel.

In the days after the fall of Jerusalem in 587 BC to the
Babylonians, the people of Israel were stunned to find that
their leaders were in exile, their capital of Jerusalem was in
ruins, and their holiest house of worship—the great temple in
Jerusalem—had been destroyed. As they contemplated their
future and prayed for salvation, God answered their prayers
and delivered them back home to Jerusalem.

He sent Nehemiah, a Jew living in Babylon, to assist in
the rebuilding efforts in Jerusalem. At that point, they found
common ground for redeveloping a closer relationship with
God: work!

Then I said to them, "You see the trouble we are in, how
Jerusalem lies in ruins with its gates burned. Come,

let us rebuild the wall of Jerusalem, so that we may no longer suffer disgrace." I told them that the hand of my God had been gracious upon me, and also the words that the king had spoken to me. Then they said, "Let us start building!" So they committed themselves to the common good.

But when Sanballat the Horonite and Tobiah the Ammonite official, and Geshem the Arab heard of it, they mocked and ridiculed us, saying, "What is this that you are doing? Are you rebelling against the king?" Then I replied to them, "The God of [H]eaven is the one who will give us success, and we his servants are going to start building . . ." (Nehemiah 2:17–20)

Nehemiah's story of the beginning of the people's efforts to rebuild Jerusalem has a couple of messages for us in modern times. First, no matter what era, country, or generation, people can come together for a cause greater than any individual in the group for the common good. Second, Nehemiah tells us that such group work projects help us fulfill God's will. God delights in our work, especially when we all work together for the common good.

If Nehemiah's group work project sounds like it could be a precursor to socialism, this project differs from a socialist effort in two ways: (1) the people are working of their own will, not because they were required to do so by a central government, and (2) through their work together in love, the people are worshiping God. The Christian Capitalist searches for opportunities that include group work projects such as these, whether it is a soup kitchen, a house for a poor or needy person, or a prison ministry. When we work together, we please God.

Those kinds of group efforts often lead to a deeper sense of community and purpose for those who participate. Nehemiah describes it beautifully: "So we rebuilt the wall, and all the wall was joined together to half its height; for the people had a mind to work" (Nehemiah 4:6). While they may have disagreed occasionally about the materials, the manner, and the scope of the rebuilding project, Nehemiah makes it clear that they found common ground through God's gift to them from the ancient times: work!

CHAPTER 2

WE ARE MADE IN GOD'S IMAGE TO GIVE

The second characteristic we know about God from Hebrew Scripture is that He is generous. He gives humans everything they need: whether it is Adam and Eve in the Garden of Eden, Noah and all the animals in the kingdom and a fresh start, or Abraham and Sarah, whose descendants outnumber the stars, we find God abundantly generous with the results of His hard work.

Because we are made in His image, we are likewise inclined to use the results of our work to benefit others. While the ancient fathers of the people of Israel were Abraham, Isaac, and Jacob, one of the earliest examples of God's abundant generosity in Hebrew Scripture comes from Jacob's son, Joseph.

Jacob had twelve sons. These men became the leaders of the twelve tribes of Israel. The youngest, Joseph, was Jacob's favorite. As is so often the case among siblings, the older brothers developed a sense of jealousy of their younger brother, and they began to despise and eventually hate Joseph.

One day, Joseph shared with his brothers that he had a dream. In the dream, he saw himself in the center of them, symbolized as a sheaf of wheat, and they all bowed down to him. He predicted that the land would have a great famine and that his brothers would rely on him for their survival. That was the final straw for the brothers; they decided then and there that their father's favorite son had to go. Instead of killing him, however, they sold him into slavery, and he was carried off to serve as a slave of Pharaoh, the king of Egypt.

God had blessed Joseph with many talents, including the gifts of management and leadership. In the house of Pharaoh, Joseph quickly became a leader in Pharaoh's inner circle and eventually a senior-level official in charge of various parts of the kingdom. That's when the opportunity for generosity arose:

> *The seven years of plenty that prevailed in the land of Egypt came to an end; and the seven years of famine began to come, just as Joseph had said. There was famine in every country, but throughout the land of Egypt there was bread. When all the land of Egypt was famished, the people cried to Pharaoh for bread. Pharaoh said to all the Egyptians, "Go to Joseph; what he says to you, do." And since the famine had spread over all the land, Joseph opened all the storehouses, and sold to the Egyptians, for the famine was severe in the land of Egypt. Moreover, all the world came to Joseph in Egypt to buy grain, because the famine became severe throughout the world. (Genesis 41:53–57)*

Joseph could have easily kept all the grain he had stored for seven years during the bountiful times and shared it only with members of Pharaoh's court. Instead, he shared it among the people of Egypt to keep them from starving. Furthermore, and most importantly, Joseph used his wealth and his management skills as an opportunity to reconcile with his brothers. When they came to him on behalf of the people of Israel, begging for mercy and for food, he shared his love and his food generously (Genesis 45:11–15).

Not only did he reconcile with his brothers after their terrible treatment of him years earlier, but Joseph also used his blessings of God to benefit the whole ancient world. Joseph understood that possessing great wealth created an opportunity to share that wealth generously. This act of abundant generosity was the direct result of God blessing Joseph, who, like all of us, was made in His image. He was made in God's image to work and to give!

This lesson of sharing abundant wealth for the good of the whole community may have gotten its first mention in the Hebrew Scripture through the story of Joseph and his brothers, but it was soon woven into the fabric of the culture of the Hebrew people. As we discussed in the previous chapter, God sent Moses to lead them out of slavery in Egypt and out into the wilderness, and the people soon began to complain about thirst and hunger. God heard their complaints and responded by providing manna from Heaven for His people. Moses told them how to consume this bread from God:

> *"This is what the Lord has commanded: 'Gather as much of it as each of you needs, an omer [a Hebrew standard of measurement] to a person according to the number of persons, all providing for those in their own tents.'" The Israelites did so, some gathering more, some*

less. But when they measured it with an omer, those who gathered much had nothing over, and those who gathered little had no shortage; they gathered as much as each of them needed. (Exodus 16:16–18)

God provided the entire nation of Israel with food in the desert through an overwhelming act of generosity. Yet, by His design, everyone's family had as much as they needed. This act of giving was both communal in its scope and, yet, personal in its impact. As a result, it created a model for giving for future generations.

Soon after, Moses, with God's instruction, began to develop new rules for the way the people would relate to each other. He wrote these new rules down in the books of the Torah, and they clearly show that God desired His people to be generous with each other, as He was generous with them.

For six years you shall sow your land and gather in its yield; but the seventh year you shall let it rest and lie fallow, so that the poor of your people may eat; and what they leave the wild animals may eat. You shall do the same with your vineyard, and with your olive orchard. Six days you shall do your work, but on the seventh day you shall rest, so that your ox and your donkey may have relief, and your homeborn slave and the resident alien may be refreshed. (Exodus 23:10–12)

These initial instructions to Moses in the wilderness became a tradition for the people of Israel. In a separate set of rules in the Torah, God told the people of Israel to share their abundance with the priests of their culture—who had no independent ability to produce for themselves—in the form of the first "widows and orphans fund":

> *Every third year you should bring out the full tithe of your produce for the year, and store it within your towns; the Levites, because they have no allotment or inheritance with you, as well as the resident aliens, the orphans, and the widows in your towns, may come and eat their fill so that the Lord your God may bless you and all the work that you undertake. (Deuteronomy 14:28–29)*

This rule from the book of Deuteronomy contains several important messages from God to His people that become the foundation for the Christian Capitalist work ethic. First, everyone should work. Second, when the work is done and on a regular basis, those who have been blessed with prosperity because of that work should share it with others. Finally, and most important for the purposes of the Christian Capitalist, God will bless the people and the work of those who work hard and share with others!

Furthermore, one of the core principles of Christian Capitalism, giving generously to the poor, is established in detail in the Torah:

> *If there is among you anyone in need, a member of your community in any of your towns within the land that the Lord your God is giving you, do not be hardhearted or tight-fisted toward your needy neighbor. You should rather open your hand, willingly lending enough to meet the need, whatever it may be.*
>
> *Be careful that you do not entertain a mean thought, thinking, "The seventh year, the year of remission, is near," and therefore view your needy neighbor with hostility and give nothing; your neighbor might cry to the Lord against you, and you would incur guilt.*

Give liberally and be ungrudging when you do so, for on this account the Lord your God will bless you in all your work and in all that you undertake.

Since there will never cease to be some in need on the Earth, I therefore command you, "Open your hand to the poor and needy neighbor in your land." (Deuteronomy 15:7–11, emphasis added)

From these verses, some of the themes of Jesus's ministry and teachings are apparent. First, everyone must work hard. Second, they are to "give liberally" to the poor since the poor are the responsibility of the rich. Finally, there will always be poor people, so this obligation to give liberally will never be fully satisfied.

The book of Leviticus renews this requirement but extends it further to include those from outside the people of Israel: "When you reap the harvest of your land, you should not repeat to the very edges of your field, or gather the gleanings of your harvest; you should leave them for the poor and for the alien: I am the Lord your God" (Leviticus 23:22). The reference to the "alien" means someone who is not native to Israel. This responsibility therefore extends to both family members and strangers: "If any of your kin fall into difficulty and become dependent on you, you shall support them; they shall live with you as though resident aliens" (Leviticus 25:35).

For those people who follow God's commands to work hard and give generously, He likewise blesses them and all the work that they do. Moses tells God's people:

Then you shall again obey the Lord, observing all his commandments that I am commanding you today, and the Lord your God will make you abundantly prosperous in all your undertakings, in the fruit of your body, in the fruit of your livestock, and in the fruit of your

soil. For the Lord will again take delight in prospering
you, just as he delighted in prospering your ancestors . . .
(Deuteronomy 30:8–9)

David, the first king of Israel, commissioned the construction
of the first temple in Jerusalem and called the entire community together. In an act of servant leadership, he both allocated
community resources and gave generously from his personal
treasure. Once he did so, the people of Israel gave freely to
provide enough materials and labor to complete the temple.
In a prayer of thanksgiving, David summarized the principle
that we are made in His image to give:

> *I know, my God, that you search the heart, and take*
> *pleasure in uprightness; in the uprightness of my heart*
> *I have freely offered all these things, and now I have*
> *seen your people, who are present here, offering freely*
> *and joyously to you.*
>
> *O Lord, the God of Abraham, Isaac, and Israel, our*
> *ancestors, keep forever such purposes and thoughts in*
> *the hearts of your people, and direct their hearts toward*
> *you. (1 Chronicles 29:17–18)*

God blesses us in the way that David prayerfully requested:
the purpose and thought of freely offering ourselves and our
belongings to God is in our hearts as we direct them to God!

CHAPTER 3

LAYING THE FOUNDATION FOR A CHRISTIAN ETHIC OF WORK AND GIVING

Hundreds of years after God gave the rules of giving to Moses, God still asked His people to be generous to each other. After Moses brought the Ten Commandments to the people of Israel, David and Solomon built the temple in Jerusalem as the first kings of a united nation. A culture of worship arose around the temple in Jerusalem. In that culture, David attributed numerous hymns called Psalms that he wrote to praise God, thank Him for His blessings, or lament the troubles that had afflicted him during his reign. Just like the older Hebrew Scriptures, the Psalms developed independent themes of work and giving.

A new theme arose at this time, as well: the insecurity of wealth compared to God's love. While wealthy people certainly lived within the people of Israel, the Psalms—and later the prophets—in this time developed the theological position that a person's financial status had moral implications. Like it, another theme developed over time: God blesses those who give generously to the poor. This theme set the table for the lessons of the Kingdom of Heaven that Jesus brought to the people of Israel hundreds of years later.

WORK ETHIC IN PSALMS AND PROVERBS

While much of the ancient Hebrew Scriptures focus on people's admiration of the works of God, many of the Psalms have a dual message when it comes to our view of God's work. On one hand, just as in ancient times, people expressed wonder at the beautiful works of God.

Praise the Lord!

I will give thanks to the Lord with my whole heart, in the company of the upright, in the congregation.

Great are the works of the Lord, studied by all who delight in them.

Full of honor and majesty is [H]is work, and [H]is righteousness endures forever.

He has gained renown by [H]is wonderful deeds; the Lord is gracious and merciful. (Psalm 111:1–4)

Furthermore, people recognized that all the Earth is God's work: "O Lord, how manifold are your works! In wisdom you have made them all; the Earth is full of your creatures" (Psalm 104:24). The people in the time of the Psalms understood their small position amid the awesomeness of God's mighty creation: "You have multiplied, O Lord my God, your wondrous deeds and your thoughts toward us; none can compare with you.

Were I to proclaim and tell of them, they would be more than can be counted" (Psalm 40:5; see also Psalm 96:1–4).

This helped the people of Israel put some sense of order into the otherwise chaotic world, with people working just a level lower than God:

> *When I look at your heavens, the work of your fingers, the moon and the stars that you have established; what are human beings that you are mindful of them, mortals that you care for them? Yet you have made them a little lower than God, and crowned them with glory and honor. You have given them dominion over the works of your hands; you have put all things under their feet. (Psalm 8:3–6)*

This respect and love of God's people likewise became a focal point for spreading the news of God to other parts of the ancient world.

> *Sing to [H]im, sing praises to [H]im; tell of all [H]is wonderful works.*
>
> *Glory in [H]is holy name; let the hearts of those who seek the Lord rejoice.*
>
> *Seek the Lord and [H]is strength; seek [H]is presence continually.*
>
> *Remember the wonderful works [H]e has done, [H]is miracles, and the judgments [H]e has uttered . . . (Psalm 105:2–5)*

This joyful attitude was also expressed in a very personal manner: "For you, O Lord, have made me glad by your work; at the works of your hands I sing for joy" (Psalm 92:4).

In some instances, this gratitude was expressed as a refrain: "Let them thank the Lord for his steadfast love, for
[H]is wonderful works to humankind" (Psalm 107:8). People
even hoped that God would rejoice in His own works: "May
the glory of the Lord endure forever; may the Lord rejoice in
[H]is works . . ." (Psalm 104:31).

On the other hand, in the Psalms that often lament a
person's misfortune, people asked God to guide their work.

Let your work be manifest to your servants,

and your glorious power to their children.

Let the favor of the Lord our God be upon us,

and prosper for us the work of our hands—

O prosper the work of our hands! (Psalm 90:16–17)

Thus, the Psalms reflected an ethic of hard work that continued from the ancient days and the traditions developed in the
Torah.

The Book of Proverbs also reflects this work ethic. God
made people to work hard and prosper: "A little sleep, a little
slumber, a little folding of the hands to rest—and poverty will
come on you like a robber, and want, like an armed warrior"
(Proverbs 24:33–34). This applies to all kinds of work: "In
all toil there is profit, but mere talk leads only to poverty"
(Proverbs 14:23). Proverbs also sets those who work hard in
contrast to those who do not: "The appetite of the lazy craves,
and gets nothing, while the appetite of the diligent is richly
supplied" (Proverbs 13:4).

Taken together, the Psalms and Proverbs show Christian
Capitalists today that God instilled an ethic of hard work in
His children because they are made in His image and because
He works hard.

THE POOR AND NEEDY

Not all workers got the same result from their labors, however. At some point after the reign of David and Solomon, the people of Israel, in the form of the twelve tribes, began to become more distant. Soon, the kingdom divided into two parts, with the northern portion led by a new king and several tribes and the tribe of Judah to the south focused on the temple culture of Jerusalem. Around 720 BC, the northern kingdom was conquered by the Assyrians. This was followed 250 years later by the invasion of the Babylonians, the ultimate fall of Jerusalem, and the destruction of the temple in 587 BC. From the end of King Solomon's reign to the fall of Jerusalem in 587 BC, the people of Israel were divided in a political and military fashion that made it easier for foreign invaders to conquer them. Biblical scholars have typically focused on these developments, as well as the spiritual wandering eye of the people who kept straying from God and following the local gods prevalent in Palestine at that time. A careful review of the Psalms, however, reveals the people of Israel were also divided based on financial status.

Once Solomon left the throne, the people of Israel became increasingly focused on issues that plague the United States today. Namely, the rich were getting richer and the poor more destitute. In particular, this concept was introduced through a phrase repeated by a number of different authors of the Psalms: poor and needy. While the development of the economy led to a class of rich people, it also had the negative consequence of developing a poor class that prayed to God for relief: "Let all who seek you rejoice and be glad in you. Let those who love your salvation say evermore, 'God is great!' But I am poor and needy; hasten to me, O God! You are my help and my deliverer; O Lord, do not delay!" (Psalm 70:4–5).

As a result, people were quick to praise God when they received His blessing: "With my mouth I will give great thanks to the Lord; I will praise [H]im in the midst of the throng. For [H]e stands at the right hand of the needy, to save them from those who would condemn them to death" (Psalm 109:30–31).

The intensity of the appeal of some of the authors reflected the desperation of their situations:

> *Incline your ear, O Lord, and answer me, for I am poor and needy. Preserve my life, for I am devoted to you; save your servant who trusts in you. You are my God; be gracious to me, O Lord, for to you do I cry all day long. (Psalm 86:1–3)*

In modern times, we often refer to the poor and needy as marginalized. In these ancient times, they were much the same: "Have regard for your covenant, for the dark places of the land are full of the haunts of violence. Do not let the downtrodden be put to shame; let the poor and needy praise your name" (Psalm 74:20–21).

Even during the early days of the Psalms, people also asked God to bless the king who helps the poor and needy: "May he defend the cause of the poor of the people, give deliverance to the needy, and crush the oppressor" (Psalm 72:4). King David and his son Solomon were likely to have been the first rulers in ancient Israel to deal with this dichotomy of rich and poor.

The Book of Proverbs likewise implores the people of Israel to help the poor and the needy: "Those who despise their neighbors are sinners, but happy are those who are kind to the poor" (Proverbs 14:21). Not only are those who help the poor happy, God will bless them: "Those who are generous are blessed, for they share their bread with the poor" (Proverbs 22:9). The flip side of the coin is also true. People who don't help the poor will be miserable: "If you close your ear to the cry of the poor, you will cry out and not be heard" (Proverbs 21:13). According to Proverbs, it can be confidently inferred that the act of tending to the poor and needy is an essential aspect of one's devotion to God.

THE EVIL OF RICHES

With the development of the "poor and needy" among the people of Israel, the tone of the Psalms takes on two themes regarding the rich: (1) the implication that people become rich through some kind of wrongdoing or evil acts and; (2) that reliance on wealth becomes an artificial replacement for trust in God. Both themes arrive at the same theological point; the poor are more righteous than the rich: "'Give justice to the weak and the orphan; maintain the right of the lowly and the destitute. Rescue the weak and the needy; deliver them from the hand of the wicked'" (Psalm 82:3–4).

One clear example from later in the Psalms of the "wicked rich" theme is based on the author's experience as a poor and needy person suffering the evil acts of a rich person. The poor and needy person asks for God's wrath against the evil person who shows no mercy to the poor: "For he did not remember to show kindness, but pursued the poor and needy and the brokenhearted to their death. . . . But you, O Lord my Lord, act on my behalf for your name's sake; because your steadfast love is good, deliver me. For I am poor and needy, and my heart is pierced within me" (Psalm 109:16, 21–22).

A second theme in the Psalms encourages rich people to take refuge in God and not in wealth: "The righteous will see, and fear, and will laugh at the evildoer, saying, 'See the one who would not take refuge in God, but trusted in abundant riches, and sought refuge in wealth!'" (Psalm 52:6–7). The Psalms clearly state that people should not trust in wealth. God repays according to their work: "Put no confidence in extortion, and set no vain hopes on robbery; if riches increase, do not set your heart on them. Once God has spoken; twice have I heard this: that power belongs to God, and steadfast love belongs to you, O Lord. For you repay to all according to their work" (Psalm 62:10–12).

One author of the Psalms goes so far as to directly con-
nect wickedness with prosperity and then thanks God that he
is still poor and needy! The wicked increase in riches, but that
becomes a slippery slope for those who seek righteousness.
Ultimately, God provides the only refuge:

> *Truly God is good to the upright, to those who are pure
> in heart.*
>
> *But as for me, my feet had almost stumbled; my steps
> had nearly slipped.*
>
> *For I was envious of the arrogant; I saw the prosperity
> of the wicked.*
>
> *And they say, "How can God know? Is there knowledge
> in the Most High?"*
>
> *Such are the wicked; always at ease, they increase in riches.*
>
> *Truly you set them in slippery places; you make them
> fall to ruin.*
>
> *How they are destroyed in a moment, swept away
> utterly by terrors!*
>
> *But for me it is good to be near God; I have made the
> Lord God my refuge, to tell of all your works. (Psalm
> 73:1–3, 11–12, 18–19, 28)*

Using an entirely different approach, another psalm author
portrays the rich and the poor as all the same in God's eyes.
As a result, everyone ends up in the same place in front of the
Lord. This line of thinking doesn't do much to compel the rich
to give to the poor, although it appears that the author's intent
is to let rich folks know that their prosperity on Earth is only
temporary. In the end, the message is similar to the way people
would phrase it today: you can't take it with you!

Hear this, all you peoples; give ear, all inhabitants of the world, both low and high, rich and poor together.

My mouth shall speak wisdom; the meditation of my heart shall be understanding.

I will incline my ear to a proverb; I will solve my riddle to the music of the harp.

Why should I fear in times of trouble, when the iniquity of my persecutors surrounds me, those who trust in their wealth and boast of the abundance of their riches?

Truly, no ransom avails for one's life, there is no price one can give to God for it.

For the ransom of life is costly, and can never suffice, that one should live on forever and never see the grave.

When we look at the wise, they die; fool and dolt perish together and leave their wealth to others.

Their graves are their homes forever, their dwelling places to all generations, though they named lands their own.

Do not be afraid when some become rich, when the wealth of their houses increases.

For when they die they will carry nothing away; their wealth will not go down after them.

Though in their lifetime they count themselves happy—for you are praised when you do well for yourself—they will go to the company of their ancestors, who will never again see the light.

Mortals cannot abide in their pomp; they are like the animals that perish. (Psalm 49:1–11, 16–20)

THE EARTHLY AND HEAVENLY BENEFITS OF GIVING

Contrary to all appearances, not all the references to the rich in the Psalms state that they are wicked. This can be seen through one simple theme throughout the Psalms: those who earn their fortune through hard work, following God's commandments, are rewarded with righteousness and blessing from God. Not only do the wealthy have a blessing that endures for generations, but they benefit from knowing that justice is served and that righteousness fills their communities. This trend started when God brought the people out of slavery in Egypt with Moses as their leader:

> *So [H]e brought [H]is people out with joy, [H]is chosen ones with singing.*
>
> *He gave them the lands of the nations, and they took possession of the wealth of the peoples, that they might keep [H]is statutes and observe [H]is laws. Praise the Lord! (Psalm 105:43–45)*

One of the early psalms encourages folks to give because it has the effect of making the giver a happy person. Paul understood this notion, as centuries later he told the people of Corinth that God loves a cheerful giver. Here, the author of the psalm connects giving to happiness, and more fundamentally, to survival: "Happy are those who consider the poor; the Lord delivers them in the day of trouble. The Lord protects them and keeps them alive; they are called happy in the land" (Psalm 41:1–2).

Around the same time, another Psalm author goes into this theme in more detail. Beyond survival and happiness, this Psalm indicates that giving to the poor leads to a closer relationship with God through righteousness. Simply put, the righteous trust in the Lord, give generously, and prosper as a result: "Trust in the Lord, and do good; so you will live in the land, and enjoy security. Take delight in the Lord, and [H]e will give you the desires of your heart. Commit your way to the Lord; trust in [H]im, and [H]e will act" (Psalm 37:3–5).

Furthermore, this righteousness goes beyond rich and poor; it belongs to those who are humble and trust in the Lord. As Jesus states centuries later in his Sermon on the Mount, "the meek shall inherit the land," but the Psalm goes further and states that the meek shall ". . . delight themselves in abundant prosperity" (Psalm 37:11). In other words, anyone who is generous will likewise prosper. Even if that prosperity is not what the believer expected or as much as they desired: "Better is a little that the righteous person has than the abundance of many wicked" (Psalm 37:16).

What makes a person wicked in the eyes of the author of Psalm 37? "The wicked borrow, and do not pay back, but **the righteous are generous and keep giving**; for those blessed by the Lord shall inherit the land, but those cursed by [H]im shall be cut off" (Psalm 37:21–22, emphasis added). The wicked, therefore, are those who default on their loans, and the implication of the author here is that they may have borrowed under false pretenses in the first place.

Likewise, the righteous lend without interest and do not crush the debtor:

> *O Lord, who may abide in your tent?*
> *Who may dwell on your holy hill?*
>
> *Those who walk blamelessly,*
> *and do what is right,*
> *and speak the truth from their heart;*
>
> *who do not lend money at interest,*
> *and do not take a bribe against the innocent.*

Those who do these things shall never be moved.
(Psalm 15:1, 2, 5)

The righteous are generous and keep giving; their place with the Lord is secure. The author takes things one step further. It is not enough to lend to the poor; the righteous who have means must give generously—always: "They are ever giving liberally and lending, and their children become a blessing. Depart from evil, and do good; so you shall abide forever" (Psalm 37:26–27). Here, the author promises that giving generously for a lifetime holds the promise of an eternity with the Lord!

Much later in the history of the people of Israel, another author of a Psalm put all these concepts together and ultimately laid the foundation for Jesus to teach these concepts in his ministry hundreds of years later. God blesses the righteous and the generous!

Praise the Lord! Happy are those who fear the Lord, who greatly delight in [H]is commandments.

Their descendants will be mighty in the land; the generation of the upright will be blessed.

Wealth and riches are in their houses, and their righteousness endures forever.

They rise in the darkness as a light for the upright; they are gracious, merciful, and righteous.

It is well with those who deal generously and lend, who conduct their affairs with justice.

For the righteous will never be moved; they will be remembered forever.

They are not afraid of evil tidings; their hearts are firm, secure in the Lord.

Their hearts are steady, they will not be afraid; in the end they will look in triumph on their foes.

They have distributed freely, they have given to the poor; their righteousness endures forever; *their horn is exalted in honor.*

The wicked see it and are angry; they gnash their teeth and melt away; the desire of the wicked comes to nothing. (Psalm 112, emphasis added)

For the righteous who follow God's law—including giving to the poor—the benefits are both Earthly and Heavenly. The Psalms and the Proverbs tell us that the righteous will benefit with prosperity and what, in modern times, we would describe as generational wealth.

The Proverbs echo this philosophy from the Psalms: wisdom favors those who bless others with their wealth. In the Proverbs, "wisdom" often speaks directly to its readers as if wisdom was a person. Wisdom's directives foreshadow the Good News preached by Jesus Christ centuries later.

Wisdom only comes to people through a closer relationship with God. When wealth follows wisdom, that means it follows those who try to do God's will.

Furthermore, their actions here on Earth ultimately lead to an eternity by the Lord's side in Heaven: "Whoever pursues righteousness and kindness finds life and honor" (Proverbs 21:21). While these concepts are based on several hundred years of Psalms, it will be a few more hundred years before Jesus ties them all together and creates the theological framework that provides the path for the Christian Capitalist.

THE PROPHETS WARN THE PEOPLE, THEN PROMISE GOD'S BLESSINGS

After David's and Solomon's time, the people of Israel once again began to stray and worship other gods. God sent prophets like Isaiah to tell the people to make their paths straight and get back into a closer relationship with Him. One of the prophets, Elisha, showed the kind of servant leadership that Moses and David had earlier. Moses led the people out of slavery in Egypt, while David led to the development of the kingdom of Israel. Elisha likewise showed an attitude of servant leadership. When he was called to work with Elijah, he took everything he had and gave it to the community to honor God: "He [Elisha] returned from following him [Elijah], took the yoke of oxen, and slaughtered them; using the equipment from the oxen, he boiled their flesh, and gave it to the people, and they ate. Then he set out and followed Elijah, and became his servant" (1 Kings 19:21). In becoming a servant of Elijah, Elisha likewise became a servant of the community.

During this time of the prophets, through the mouth of Isaiah, God spoke to the people of Israel and required them to treat each other well:

> *Is not this the fast that I choose: to loose the bonds of injustice, to undo the thongs of the yoke, to let the oppressed go free, and to break every yoke? Is it not to share your bread with the hungry, and bring the homeless poor into your house; when you see the naked, to cover them, and not to hide yourself from your own kin? Then your light shall break forth like the dawn, and your healing shall spring up quickly; your vindicator shall go before you, the glory of the Lord shall be your rear guard. Then you shall call, and the Lord will answer; you shall cry for help, and he will say, Here I am.*

> *If you remove the yoke from among you, the pointing of the finger, the speaking of evil,* ***if you offer your food to the hungry and satisfy the needs of the afflicted, then your light shall rise in the darkness and your gloom be like the noonday.***

The Lord will guide you continually and satisfy your needs in parched places, and make your bones strong; and you shall be like a watered garden, like a spring of water, whose waters never fail. Your ancient ruins shall be rebuilt; you shall raise up the foundations of many generations; you shall be called the repairer of the breach, the restorer of streets to live in. (Isaiah 58:6–14, emphasis added)

Although the message of Isaiah was fundamentally one of rebuking and repentance, God still held forth to his people that he would bless them if they only took care of each other. Note in the preceding passage that God is essentially offering a new covenant to the people of Israel, that if those who have riches share it with the poor, He will provide His blessing to them. God makes a fairly straightforward offer to the lost people of Israel: "be good to others, and I will be good to you."

The prophet Micah puts it in the context of developing a relationship with God. From Micah's perspective, showing your acts of mercy to another actually brings one closer to God. That takes the message from simple "rule following" to one of salvation. This is reiterated and reframed by God's only son, Jesus Christ, years later:

He has told you, O mortal, what is good; and what does the Lord require of you but to do justice, and to love kindness, and to walk humbly with your God? (Micah 6:8)

Micah describes a closer relationship with God based on a person's work to act justly and show mercy to the needy. The prophet Zechariah delivered a message to the people of Israel that was similar to Micah's: "Thus says the Lord of hosts: Render true judgments, show kindness and mercy to one another; do not oppress the widow, the orphan, the alien, or the poor" (Zechariah 7:9–10).

Another prophet, Amos, warns the people of Israel that greed and selfishness violate God's will and sets them apart from God:

> *Therefore, because you trample on the poor and take from them levies of grain, you have built houses of hewn stone, but you shall not live in them; you have planted pleasant vineyards, but you shall not drink their wine. For I know how many are your transgressions, and how great are your sins—you who afflict the righteous, who take a bribe, and push aside the needy in the gate. . . . Seek good and not evil, that you may live; and so the Lord, the God of hosts, will be with you, just as you have said.* **Hate evil and love good, and establish justice in the gate;** *it may be that the Lord, the God of hosts, will be gracious to the remnant of Joseph. (Amos 5:11–15, emphasis added)*

The gate was likely a physical place in the ancient communities that allowed the rich to walk past the poor on a daily basis. "Pushing aside the needy at the gate," therefore, meant that rich people literally moved the poor people out of the way as they walked through it. The term people use today, marginalized, means the same thing: moving the poor out of the way so that they can't be seen or heard. The reward of caring for the poor is clear in Amos's mind: establishing justice at the gate leads to God's grace.

> *This is what the Lord God showed me—a basket of summer fruit.*
>
> *He said, "Amos, what do you see?" And I said, "A basket of summer fruit." Then the Lord said to me, "The end has come upon my people Israel; I will never again pass them by. The songs of the temple shall become wailings*

in that day," says the Lord God; "the dead bodies shall be many, cast out in every place. Be silent!"

Hear this, you that trample on the needy, and bring to ruin the poor of the land . . . (Amos 8:1-4)

Job, the prophet famous for his long suffering, likewise taught the people of Israel to help the poor by recounting God's approval of his actions: "When the ear heard, it commended me, and when the eye saw, it approved; because I delivered the poor who cried, and the orphan who had no helper. The blessing of the wretched came upon me, and I caused the widow's heart to sing for joy. . . . I was a father to the needy, and I championed the cause of the stranger" (Job 29:11–13; 16). Job describes a time when he was in a closer relationship with God, before his trials and tribulations, and it showed the people of Israel the kind of conduct that God rewards.

In a final message to Christian Capitalists in the future, the prophet Isaiah foretells the development of a new covenant and a new Kingdom of Heaven that will be brought to the world through the Word of God incarnate, his son Jesus Christ.

For I am about to create new heavens and a new Earth; the former things shall not be remembered or come to mind. . . .

They shall build houses and inhabit them; they shall plant vineyards and eat their fruit. . . . for like the days of a tree shall the days of my people be, and my chosen shall long enjoy the work of their hands.

. . . I will extend prosperity to her [Jerusalem] like a river, and the wealth of the nations like an overflowing stream . . . (Isaiah 65:17, 21–22; 66:12)

In the world of the new covenant between God and His people, in which all things are created new again, the wealth of the world is shared by the children of God with each other. In a phrase harkened later by the great capitalist economist, Adam Smith, in his masterpiece *The Wealth of Nations*, Isaiah predicts a world in which people accumulate wealth from God and work hard to give generously to each other!

PART II

JESUS TEACHES A NEW WAY TO THINK ABOUT WORKING AND GIVING

CHAPTER 4

JESUS TEACHES US ABOUT THE KINGDOM OF HEAVEN

Jesus's ministry centered primarily on the dissemination of the Good News, instructing individuals about the Kingdom of Heaven, God's affection for His children, and the importance of loving one another. Many of His teachings used financial examples as part of the lesson. While the Torah and previous teachings on money focused on how the people of Israel should work and share the blessings of God with others, they did not focus on how money and riches could impact a person's relationship with God. This theme developed in the Psalms, and Jesus took that theme and made it a key component of His teachings.

First, Jesus teaches His apostles and followers that the Kingdom of Heaven is worth everything they have. In addition to the message that God will go to great lengths to save people who have strayed from Him, Jesus likewise teaches that people should give everything up for God. His love for everyone is so precious and is such an awesome gift that they must be ready to part with everything they have to receive it.

Jesus uses two examples in the Gospel of Matthew to illustrate this point. First, He tells His apostles and followers, "The Kingdom of Heaven is like treasure hidden in a field, which someone found and hid; then in his joy he goes and sells all that he has and buys that field" (Matthew 13:44). Second, He puts people in the role of what today we would call a commercial buyer, "Again, the Kingdom of Heaven is like a merchant in search of fine pearls; on finding one pearl of great value, he went and sold all that he had and bought it" (Matthew 13:45). Talk about having a friend in the jewelry business! The pearl is that God's abundant love in the Kingdom of Heaven is so valuable that it is worth everything the merchant had!

Second, when people stray from God, Jesus tells us that He will go to great lengths to find us and bring us back into the Kingdom of Heaven. The three main stories that relate to this theme are found in the Gospel of Luke, and they are each based on parables that involve the same theme: the loss of something valuable.

PARABLES OF LOSS

In His role as a teacher of the apostles and followers, Jesus was revered by those who followed Him. They used the term *rabbi*, which was commonplace at the time, referring to a learned individual who is an expert in Holy Scripture. As a rabbi, Jesus used a powerful tool in His teaching called the parable. The parable is simply another way of referring to a story that illustrates a spiritual principle. Rather than lay out spiritual principles to His people as a code of conduct or commandments, like His predecessors, Jesus used stories to illustrate the example of the principle He was trying to teach.

When it came time to discuss the concept of the Kingdom of Heaven, Jesus frequently used these parables in His teachings. Specifically in the Gospel of Luke, Jesus employed three parables to explore the profound bond between God and His children, expressing His delight when someone is reconciled with Him. For the purposes of this book, these parables are significant because Jesus discusses God's love for His children from an economic perspective.

Today, these parables are referred to generally as the parables of loss. In each story, a person has a thing or a relationship of value that has been lost. When they find it, they are overwhelmed with joy. Jesus uses these examples to show His apostles and followers how much God values His children and wants to be in a closer relationship with them.

From the Christian Capitalist point of view, they also have an important value. When Jesus talks about God's love, He is telling people that God values a relationship with them. In telling these parables, Jesus uses objects or people to illustrate that value. In each of the parables of loss, Jesus indicates to His apostles and followers that, if God were personified, each of them would be the most valuable thing He owned, and He would celebrate if they were lost and then found!

The Lost Sheep

Jesus first tells a parable involving loss that reveals God's generous love in allowing people to come back into a closer relationship with Him. In it, Jesus portrays God as a shepherd who has lost one of his flock of sheep.

> *Which one of you, having a hundred sheep and losing one of them, does not leave the ninety-nine in the wilderness and go after the one that is lost until he finds it? When he has found it, he lays it on his shoulders and rejoices. And when he comes home, he calls together his*

friends and neighbors, saying to them, "Rejoice with me, for I have found my sheep that was lost." Just so, I tell you, there will be more joy in [H]eaven over one sinner who repents than over ninety-nine righteous persons who need no repentance. (Luke 15:4–7)

In ancient Israel, the economy was built primarily on agriculture. Jesus regularly tells stories among the olive groves and the vineyards of Judea, and he certainly focuses on the economic importance of the Sea of Galilee for His first four apostles (Peter, Andrew, James, and John were all fishermen). Livestock likewise held significant value in those days. Sheep, in particular, were a common source of examples for Jesus in parables. In comparing Himself to a good shepherd, Jesus not only emphasizes God's love for people but also the importance that people hold with God. While people today tend to think of sheep as simple commodities, in those days, they were valuable assets.

The parable of the lost sheep illustrates this in statistical terms. Jesus compares God to a shepherd, who loses one sheep out of a flock of one hundred. Even with 99 percent of the sheep secure, the shepherd goes after the 1 percent, the lone missing sheep, to ensure its safety. Likewise, God will seek people out to protect them and return them to a closer relationship with Him. By returning to the flock, the 1 percent are able to enter into the Kingdom of Heaven.

This parable also has an ironic element to it. Not only does Jesus compare the value of a person's soul to God as the value that people put on belongings, but He tells everyone that it is also appropriate to feel joy when they find something of value that they lost. Instead of admonishing His apostles and followers to give something away or let it go, His stories illustrate that people should pursue things of value just as God pursues His children, because they are valuable.

The Lost Coin

After comparing God to a good shepherd, Jesus then tells everyone that if a woman loses a coin, she will move aside everything and sweep the floors to look for that lost coin, even if it is only one of ten. Then, upon finding the coin, she will tell all her neighbors and rejoice at finding that lost token.

> *Or what woman having ten silver coins, if she loses one of them, does not light a lamp, sweep the house, and search carefully until she finds it? When she has found it, she calls together her friends and neighbors, saying, "Rejoice with me, for I have found the coin that I had lost." Just so, I tell you, there is joy in the presence of the angels of God over one sinner who repents. (Luke 15:8–10)*

What are we to make of this? Didn't Jesus also tell everyone that they had to give everything away? Now, He tells the story of the woman who finds one coin and rejoices. If she is one of His followers, why would she even care if she lost the coin?

As is so often the case in the Gospels, Jesus shows everyone in the stories that He is not an economist, a manager, or a foreman of workers. He is the Messiah sent to help everyone find the path to a closer relationship with God and eventual entrance into the Kingdom of Heaven.

In telling the story of the parable of the lost coin, Jesus is not telling everyone to scrimp and save and then rejoice if they manage to recover a lost coin. While that is certainly fine, the point of the story is to tell everyone that God's love extends even to those who have lost their way and follow the path of sin that leads them away from Him.

In modern terms, people think of sin as some action that is either immoral or somehow not within the standards of fine, upstanding Christian behavior. Las Vegas is known as Sin City because it provides plenty of ways to get into trouble along these lines! For the Christian Capitalist, the real Sin City is a desolate place because it's far from God's love. The original meaning of sin is separation, or distance, from God. It doesn't have to do so much with actions as it does our beliefs and what we feel in our hearts. That's why when people confess their sins, they ask for forgiveness both for things they have done and left undone. If people repent and return to God and His ways, He will rejoice, like the woman who found the lost coin.

For the Christian Capitalist, however, the parable of the lost coin holds double meaning. If people are sinners and lose their way from a closer relationship with God, they are like the lost coin: God will rejoice once they return to Him and are found. For the Christian Capitalist, recognition of the separation from God is the first step in returning to that relationship. The second step, however, is just as important: how people can use the coins they have and recognize their gifts from God to assist them in returning to that relationship. Time and time again, both the Psalms and the Gospels compel people to give to the poor and share the blessings that they have with the world. It is God's way. So the next time a person finds a coin they have lost, they can give some thought to this parable and then give that coin to someone who needs it!

The Prodigal Son

In the third parable of loss, Jesus tells everyone about a son who took his inheritance before his father's death and spent it all while living a sinful life. Then Jesus said:

> *There was a man who had two sons. The younger of them said to his father, "Father, give me the share of the property that will belong to me." So he divided his property between them.*

A few days later the younger son gathered all he had and traveled to a distant country, and there he squandered his property in dissolute living.

When he had spent everything, a severe famine took place throughout that country, and he began to be in need. So he went and hired himself out to one of the citizens of that country, who sent him to his fields to feed the pigs. He would gladly have filled himself with the pods that the pigs were eating; and no one gave him anything.

But when he came to himself he said, "How many of my father's hired hands have bread enough and to spare, but here I am dying of hunger! I will get up and go to my father, and I will say to him, 'Father, I have sinned against heaven and before you; I am no longer worthy to be called your son; treat me like one of your hired hands.'"

So he set off and went to his father. But while he was still far off, his father saw him and was filled with compassion; he ran and put his arms around him and kissed him.

Then the son said to him, "Father, I have sinned against heaven and before you; I am no longer worthy to be called your son."

But the father said to his slaves, "Quickly, bring out a robe—the best one—and put it on him; put a ring on his finger and sandals on his feet. And get the fatted calf and kill it, and let us eat and celebrate; for this son of mine was dead and is alive again; he was lost and is found!" And they began to celebrate.

Now his elder son was in the field; and when he came and approached the house, he heard music and dancing. He called one of the slaves and asked what was going on.

He replied, "Your brother has come, and your father has killed the fatted calf, because he has got him back safe and sound."

Then he became angry and refused to go in. His father came out and began to plead with him. But he answered his father, "Listen! For all these years I have been working like a slave for you, and I have never disobeyed your command; yet you have never given me even a young goat so that I might celebrate with my friends. But when this son of yours came back, who has devoured your property with prostitutes, you killed the fatted calf for him!"

Then the father said to him, "Son, you are always with me, and all that is mine is yours.

But we had to celebrate and rejoice, because this brother of yours was dead and has come to life; he was lost and has been found." (Luke 15:11–32)

The parable of the Prodigal Son may be one of the most famous stories that Jesus told. Two thousand years later, people around the world refer to a person returning to a family or community after an extended period as a "prodigal son." In ancient Israel, the highest position a man could have in a family was the father, followed by the firstborn son. The second son held a share of the inheritance but knew that his older brother would not only have the lion's share of the inheritance but also would likely take over the operation of that family's business as well.

In this story, the younger son demands his inheritance before his father has passed away. While unusual, this was not uncommon in ancient times. The father, while disagreeing with the second son's approach, grants his wish. He gives the second son his share of the inheritance and sends him on his way with his blessing. The second son blows it all away. He eventually finds himself at rock bottom, and wishing that he had as much to eat as the pigs on the farm where he works, he returns home to beg for mercy from his father.

While the first son is not too happy about his brother's return, the father's joy at having the second son return home is overwhelming. He puts his finest robe on the prodigal son and prepares a huge feast to celebrate his return. The economics of this lesson are significant.

First, Jesus compares the Kingdom of Heaven to an inheritance that is freely given simply because we are human. That inheritance is available for everyone to take, but they must manage it and care for it. Like the prodigal son, if people waste the opportunity, they end up far from God and in dire straits. Second, when people return to God and have a close relationship with Him, God is overwhelmed with joy. From a financial perspective, the father figure in the story lavishes gifts and a feast on the returning son. These financial examples illustrate the joy that God shows when one of His children returns to him.

Once again, instead of telling His apostles and followers that the Prodigal Son was worthless or that they shouldn't worry about the material possessions that the father used to celebrate the son's return, Jesus emphasized how those belongings were used to celebrate love. The Prodigal Son story wouldn't have near the impact if the father in this parable had given everything away, as Jesus later instructs some of his rich followers to do!

In summary, the three parables of loss have three significant implications for the Christian Capitalists. First, they indicate that the Kingdom of Heaven has value in human economic terms and that it is difficult for people to put into perspective. No matter how many material belongings people have, what kind of property they own, and how much is in their bank accounts, God views all of it as insignificant compared to the value of His children's souls. When we sin and become distant from Him, He is overjoyed when we return to Him!

The second implication is the flip side of the proverbial coin: no matter how much wealth people accumulate, none of it matters compared to the value of the Kingdom of Heaven and being in a closer relationship with God. In fact, Jesus will later tell the rich that their wealth is interfering with their ability to follow Him on His path. This is the careful balance that the Christian Capitalist has to follow. While working hard to accumulate wealth, the Christian Capitalist has to keep that wealth in perspective and ensure that it is shared with the poor and the needy.

Finally, Jesus regularly compares God and His sense of loss over His children when they stray away from Him to people who lose their most valuable possessions: from a sheep or a coin with tangible value to a son whose value cannot be measured. In each case, the person experiences anxiety and grief over the loss, then pure joy with the return! Jesus uses economic examples in these parables to show the value that God places on His children.

THE PARABLE OF THE TALENTS

One of the most vivid financial analogies Jesus creates in any parable is the Parable of the Talents. To modern ears, it makes everyone uncomfortable to hear about a master dealing with his slaves. In the context of the time, however, Jesus used this relationship to show how subservient all people are to God.

More importantly, He compared the Good News to a measurement of financial currency used at the time (talents) and taught His apostles and followers that they were responsible for both caring for the talents and growing them. As Jesus explained later, the talent is an analogy to the Good News, which every Christian is responsible for spreading:

For it is as if a man, going on a journey, summoned his slaves and entrusted his property to them; to one he gave five talents, to another two, to another one, to each according to his ability. Then he went away.

The one who had received the five talents went off at once and traded with them, and made five more talents. In the same way, the one who had the two talents made two more talents. But the one who had received the one talent went off and dug a hole in the ground and hid his master's money.

After a long time the master of those slaves came and settled accounts with them.

Then the one who had received the five talents came forward, bringing five more talents, saying, "Master, you handed over to me five talents; see, I have made five more talents."

His master said to him, "Well done, good and trustworthy slave; you have been trustworthy in a few things, I will put you in charge of many things; enter into the joy of your master."

And the one with the two talents also came forward, saying, "Master, you handed over to me two talents; see, I have made two more talents." His master said to him, "Well done, good and trustworthy slave; you have been trustworthy in a few things, I will put you in charge of many things; enter into the joy of your master."

Then the one who had received the one talent also came forward, saying, "Master, I knew that you were a harsh man, reaping where you did not sow, and gathering where you did not scatter seed; so I was afraid, and I went and hid your talent in the ground. Here you have what is yours."

But his master replied, "You wicked and lazy slave! You knew, did you, that I reap where I did not sow, and gather where I did not scatter? Then you ought to have invested my money with the bankers, and on my return I would have received what was my own with interest. So take the talent from him, and give it to the one with the ten talents. **For to all those who have, more will be given, and they will have an abundance;** *but from those who have nothing, even what they have will be taken away. As for this worthless slave, throw him into the outer darkness, where there will be weeping and gnashing of teeth." (Matthew 25:14–30, emphasis added)*

For the Christian Capitalist, this parable has a dual meaning. First, Christian Capitalists are responsible for spreading the Good News and growing the faith around the world. Second, if Jesus uses growth and investments as an analogy for spreading the Gospel around the world, He likewise expects those who have been blessed by God to invest and grow the blessings that God has given them. As Jesus concludes, to those who have been given blessings, more will come.

THE PARABLE OF THE SOWER OF THE SEED

While Jesus was teaching the apostles and followers about the Kingdom of Heaven, He was also instructing them about how to teach the word on their own. As He was telling the apostles about the kinds of people who would hear the word, He divided them into three groups: (1) those who would hear the word; (2) those who would hear, and not follow, after some kind of trial and tribulation; and (3) those who would not receive the word at all.

When a great crowd gathered and people from town after town came to him, He said in a parable:

> *A sower went out to sow his seed; and as he sowed, some fell on the path and was trampled on, and the birds of the air ate it up. Some fell on the rock; and as it grew up, it withered for lack of moisture. Some fell among thorns, and the thorns grew with it and choked it. Some fell into good soil, and when it grew, it produced a hundredfold. As he said this, he called out, "Let anyone with ears to hear listen!"*

> *Then [H]is disciples asked him what this parable meant. He said, "To you it has been given to know the secrets of the [K]ingdom of God; but to others I speak in parables, so that 'looking they may not perceive, and listening they may not understand.' Now the parable is this: The seed is the [W]ord of God. The ones on the path are those who have heard; then the devil comes and takes away the [W]ord from their hearts, so that they may not believe and be saved. The ones on the rock are those who, when they hear the [W]ord, receive it with joy. But these have no root; they believe only for a while and in a time of testing fall away. As for what fell among the thorns, these are the ones who hear; but as they go on their way,* **they are choked by the cares and riches and pleasures of life**, *and their fruit does not mature. But as for that in the good soil, these are the ones who, when they hear the [W]ord, hold it fast in an honest and good heart, and bear fruit with patient endurance." (Luke 8:4–15, emphasis added; see also Mark 4:1–20)*

In this second group, Jesus also passes along an important and new theological concept that follows from the Psalms:

that wealth can interfere with a relationship with God. In Matthew's version, this parable ends with both a promise of benefit and a message of foreboding: "For to those who have, more will be given, and they will have an abundance; but from those who have nothing, even what they have will be taken away" (Matthew 13:12).

Matthew refers to the deceitfulness of riches, Luke describes the dynamic as being distracted by wealth, and Mark warns against the lure of wealth. Regardless of the way it is phrased in the Gospels, Jesus makes it clear that material belongings, especially for those who are wealthy, can interfere with their ability to hear the Word of the Lord. The Christian Capitalist understands, therefore, that in order to avoid these problems that Jesus describes, they have to use wealth to spread the Word!

PARABLE OF THE VINEYARD OWNER'S SON

Jesus told the parable of the vineyard owner's son to His apostles and followers to emphasize that they risk losing the gift that God has given them. While the violence of this story is shocking to modern eyes, Jesus describes a business relationship gone horribly wrong in a relatable way to His audience. Jesus tells everyone this story about the landlord–tenant relationship in an agrarian setting, one He knew they would all appreciate.

> *He began to tell the people this parable: "A man planted a vineyard, and leased it to tenants, and went to another country for a long time. When the season came, he sent a slave to the tenants in order that they might give him his share of the produce of the vineyard; but the tenants beat him and sent him away empty-handed.*

Next he sent another slave; that one also they beat and insulted and sent away empty-handed. And he sent still a third; this one also they wounded and threw out.

"Then the owner of the vineyard said, 'What shall I do? I will send my beloved son; perhaps they will respect him.' But when the tenants saw him, they discussed it among themselves and said, 'This is the heir; let us kill him so that the inheritance may be ours.' So they threw him out of the vineyard and killed him. What then will the owner of the vineyard do to them? He will come and destroy those tenants and give the vineyard to others. When they heard this, they said, 'Heaven forbid!'" (Luke 20:9–16)

The vineyard owner in this story is God, and the vineyard is the Kingdom of Heaven. The first two representatives that God sent to the kingdom were met with violence as the people rejected them. In many ways, this is how the people of Israel responded to the prophets that God sent them centuries earlier. As God reached for solutions, He sent his **beloved son** on the third attempt. The result? The ungrateful tenants of the vineyard rejected Jesus and killed Him.

Jesus tells this parable for two reasons: (1) He uses a common business relationship to create a metaphor for the Kingdom of Heaven that was relatable to His audience, and (2) He wanted to give them the not-so-subtle message: take care of the gift that God has given you, or He will find someone else who will!

PARABLE OF THE WICKED SLAVE

The parable of the vineyard owner and his son is mirrored in the parable of the wicked slave. Just as in the vineyard story, Jesus uses a business relationship to create a metaphor for the

Kingdom of Heaven. Just as in the vineyard, the key figure in this story is a wealthy person who leaves others in charge of his estate. Here, instead of a vineyard, the nobleman trusts his workers with funds and expects them to invest and grow those amounts in his absence.

> *As they were listening to this, [H]e went on to tell a parable, because [H]e was near Jerusalem, and because they supposed that the [K]ingdom of God was to appear immediately. So [H]e said, "A nobleman went to a distant country to get royal power for himself and then return. He summoned ten of his slaves, and gave them ten pounds, and said to them, 'Do business with these until I come back.' But the citizens of his country hated him and sent a delegation after him, saying, 'We do not want this man to rule over us.'*
>
> *"When he returned, having received royal power, he ordered these slaves, to whom he had given the money, to be summoned so that he might find out what they had gained by trading. The first came forward and said, 'Lord, your pound has made ten more pounds.' He said to him, 'Well done, good slave! Because you have been trustworthy in a very small thing, take charge of ten cities.' Then the second came, saying, 'Lord, your pound has made five pounds.' He said to him, 'And you, rule over five cities.'*
>
> *"Then the other came, saying, 'Lord, here is your pound. I wrapped it up in a piece of cloth, for I was afraid of you, because you are a harsh man; you take what you did not deposit, and reap what you did not sow.' He said to him, 'I will judge you by your own words, you wicked slave! You knew, did you, that I was a harsh man, taking what I did not deposit and reaping what*

*I did not sow? Why then did you not put my money
into the bank? Then when I returned, I could have collected it with interest.' He said to the bystanders, 'Take
the pound from him and give it to the one who has
ten pounds.' (And they said to him, 'Lord, he has ten
pounds!') 'I tell you, to all those who have, more will be
given; but from those who have nothing, even what they
have will be taken away.'["] (Luke 19:11–26)*

Jesus tells this lesson to His apostles and followers to yet again
emphasize that the gift of entry into the Kingdom of Heaven
is one that God gives freely but that it can also be taken away
if it is not appreciated. The Christian Capitalist sees the parable of the wicked slave and the parable of the workers in the
vineyard as important lessons for two reasons. First, Jesus frequently used business relationships and terms to create meta-
phors for His followers to help them understand the nature of
the Kingdom of Heaven. Today, we still appreciate the risk
that a business owner takes when they leave a thriving successful operation in the hands of others. Those who take care
of the business are rewarded, and those who do not grow it or
appreciate it are let go.

Second, both these parables show people that God expects
His children not only to take care of the gifts He has freely
given but to grow them as well. In particular, the parable of
the wicked slave practically demands that Christian Capitalists
invest the funds that they have earned in a business and reward
those who have assisted them in growing those investments!

RICH MAN THROUGH THE EYE
OF THE NEEDLE

For the first time, Jesus takes the teachings of all the laws of
Moses and the prophets and ties them into one simple message:

wealth can interfere with our relationship with God and our ability to enter into the Kingdom of Heaven. In the parables, where Jesus talks about how the Word of God can spread, He compares the Word of God to a seed that has various potential outcomes. Only those who hear the Word, and live according to the Word, can enter into the Kingdom of Heaven. Teaching His disciples this lesson, Jesus specifically mentions the deceitfulness of riches. While this theme is first introduced in the Psalms, Jesus puts a fine point on it in His teachings. Those who fall victim to the deceitfulness of riches cannot have a closer relationship with God and enter into the Kingdom of Heaven. Jesus tells a certain ruler to sell all his possessions:

> *A certain ruler asked him, "Good Teacher, what must I do to inherit eternal life?" Jesus said to him, "Why do you call me good? No one is good but God alone. You know the commandments: 'You shall not commit adultery; You shall not murder; You shall not steal; You shall not bear false witness; Honor your father and mother.'" He replied, "I have kept all these since my youth."*

> *When Jesus heard this, [H]e said to him, "There is still one thing lacking. Sell all that you own and distribute the money to the poor, and you will have treasure in heaven; then come, follow me." But when he heard this, he became sad; for he was very rich. Jesus looked at him and said, "How hard it is for those who have wealth to enter the [K]ingdom of God!* **Indeed, it is easier for a camel to go through the eye of a needle than for someone who is rich to enter the [K]ingdom of God."**

> *Those who heard it said, "Then who can be saved?" He replied, "What is impossible for mortals is possible for God." Then Peter said, "Look, we have left our homes and followed you." And [H]e said to them, "Truly I tell*

you, there is no one who has left house or wife or brothers or parents or children, for the sake of the [K]ingdom of God, who will not get back very much more in this age, and in the age to come eternal life." (Luke 18:18–30, emphasis added; see also Matthew 19:23–24 and Mark 10:23–27)

For two thousand years, people have been trying to make sense of Jesus's statement to His apostles and followers that it is easier for the camel to pass through the eye of the needle than it is for the rich man to enter into the Kingdom of Heaven. Two schools of thought have arisen over the years. First, historians and archaeologists note that in the old city of Jerusalem, the eye of the needle was a particularly small gate in an otherwise giant, insurmountable wall around the city of Jerusalem. The gate served the dual purposes of allowing human foot traffic and maintaining the integrity of the defensive walls of the city. Because a full-grown camel could measure eight feet tall at the top of its hump, the eye of the needle could only be traversed by one who got so low that it was basically kneeling. The people of Jesus's time would have recognized that the camel simply could not do it.

The other school of thought is that Jesus was referring to a sewing needle, whose eye measures no more than a fraction of an inch. It's completely impossible for a human, much less a camel, to pass through the eye of the needle. Because Jesus made this comment to his apostles and followers in the context of telling a rich man to sell all his possessions, many pastors and biblical scholars have adopted the notion that Jesus is using a metaphor. Without giving away all his possessions, the rich man has no chance of getting into heaven, just as a camel has no chance of passing through the eye of a sewing needle.

The Christian Capitalist can be in either school of thought. While appreciating the historical, archaeological, biblical, and pastoral implications of Jesus's statement about the rich man and the Kingdom of Heaven, the Christian Capitalist focuses on what comes next. Matthew, Mark, and Luke all have some version of the story in their Gospels. While each of them includes the warning to the rich man that it is easier for a camel to pass through the eye of the needle than for him to get into heaven, the Christian Capitalist focuses on Jesus's final statement to everyone who is gathered there: all things are possible with God!

Finally, while the implication of Jesus's story is that the rich man is too selfish to enter into the Kingdom of Heaven, the Christian Capitalist understands that the wealth he possesses comes from God and must be shared with others in the name of God. Only in this way can the rich man enter into the Kingdom of Heaven.

YOU CAN'T TAKE IT WITH YOU

Modern Americans spend millions of dollars on resources to assist them with their investments. The financial services industry, even in the tumultuous post-COVID-19 economy, is booming. From advisors to books and blogs, Americans have saved and invested billions and are ready to put their money toward making more money. This all has to be taken into perspective, however.

For example, when Jesus is preaching and teaching around Judah, a man asks Him to help resolve a dispute against his brother over an inheritance. Jesus warns of putting too much value on possession: "Someone in the crowd said to [H]im, 'Teacher, tell my brother to divide the family inheritance with me.' But [H]e said to him, 'Friend, who set me to be a judge or arbitrator over you?' And [H]e said to them, 'Take care! Be on your guard against all kinds of greed; for one's life does not consist in the abundance of possessions'" (Luke 12:13–15).

Maybe the most graphic example of putting wealth into perspective is found in the parable that Jesus tells of the rich man who builds barns for himself. After growing his business and generating wealth, the rich man decides to build additional barns for his grain. This is the modern equivalent of opening up new investment accounts to diversify a portfolio or expand investment interests into new ventures. Jesus gives his apostles and followers, as well as people two thousand years later, a startling message: You can't take it with you, so avoid putting riches over God.

> *Then [H]e told them a parable: "The land of a rich man produced abundantly. And he thought to himself, 'What should I do, for I have no place to store my crops?' Then he said, 'I will do this: I will pull down my barns and build larger ones, and there I will store all my grain and my goods. And I will say to my soul, Soul, you have ample goods laid up for many years; relax, eat, drink, be merry.' But God said to him, 'You fool! This very night your life is being demanded of you. And the things you have prepared, whose will they be?' 'So it is with those who store up treasures for themselves but are not rich toward God.'" (Luke 12:16–21)*

After telling everyone this parable, Jesus ultimately returns to the same message that started off our discussion of economics and the Kingdom of Heaven. The Kingdom of Heaven comes first; material possessions do not. Therefore, this means people are free not to worry about money or what they own, for it is not of priority in the first place: "He said to his disciples, 'Therefore I tell you, do not worry about your life, what you will eat, or about your body, what you will wear. For life is more than food, and the body more than clothing'" (Luke 12:22–23).

In another financial parable, the dishonest manager allows Jesus to compare worldly riches to the Heavenly riches of the Kingdom of Heaven. In preparing to lose his job because he has defrauded his master, the manager fraudulently marks down amounts that various people owe his boss. Instead of anger, the rich man applauds the dishonest manager for his actions: "And his master commended the dishonest manager because he had acted shrewdly; for the children of this age are more shrewd in dealing with their own generation than are the children of light. And I tell you, make friends for yourselves by means of dishonest wealth so that when it is gone, they may welcome you into the eternal homes" (Luke 16:8–9).

This parable is one of the most difficult to interpret because, on its face, it sounds like Jesus is either telling his apostles and followers that they should make money dishonestly or, alternatively, make friends with those who have. While Jesus certainly embraces spending time with sinners during His time on Earth, including tax collectors and prostitutes, He never really makes a case for hanging out with those who commit fraud! Having said that, the key to this parable may simply be that Earthly riches are deceitful. As we have discussed earlier in this book, the Psalms say that the wealth that people have gotten dishonestly will eventually evaporate. At that point, Christians will be glad to have made friends with those people who are dishonest so that they can introduce them to the true riches of heaven.

Furthermore, the Christian Capitalist takes two important lessons from this parable. First, being generous to others, even if that generosity may involve the belongings of others, is appropriate. It certainly is not always the case, but Jesus in this parable seems to be contending that the end justifies the means.

Second, people will frequently be deceitful toward each other. When Jesus talks about people dealing shrewdly with each other in this generation, as opposed to the children of light, the Christian Capitalist recognizes that the goal is to walk as a child of the light, as the great hymn says. Christian Capitalists leave that deceitfulness and shrewd dealing to others and, instead, welcome those who may have gained wealth when it is all gone.

YOU *REALLY* CAN'T TAKE IT WITH YOU

Jesus was a teacher, a preacher, a minister, and a prophet. While He used the story of the rich man building barns to warn people that they should not let wealth interfere with their relationship with God, He takes it one step further in telling His apostles and followers about how the Son of Man will come again to judge the living and the dead. He recalls the fire and brimstone end of the sinful cities of Sodom and Gomorrah. In telling everyone that wealth should not interfere with their relationships with God, He warns them to be ready to enter into the Kingdom of Heaven and not allow possessions to literally interfere with that transition. It is a modern cliché, but in this parable, Jesus literally is saying that "you can't take it with you"!

> *Likewise, just as it was in the days of Lot: they were eating and drinking, buying and selling, planting and building, but on the day that Lot left Sodom, it rained fire and sulfur from heaven and destroyed all of them— it will be like that on the day that the Son of Man is revealed. On that day, anyone on the housetop who has belongings in the house must not come down to take them away; and likewise anyone in the field must not turn back. Remember Lot's wife. (Luke 17:28–32)*

This final message of the parable is an important one because everyone in the crowd knew the story: as Lot led his family to escape the destruction of Sodom, his wife turned back to look at their old life, old property, and old possessions. Because she turned away from the future, she was turned into a pillar of salt! Jesus knew that everyone in the crowd knew the story, so this last three-word warning really packed a punch. "Remember Lot's wife" is another way of saying that when the Son of Man comes again, people shouldn't look back and try to grab their possessions. Those who return for their belongings may not be able to enter the Kingdom of Heaven.

CHAPTER 5

JESUS TEACHES US ABOUT WORK

Like us, Jesus Christ was born into life as a human. Unlike us, He became incarnate from the Virgin Mary and was made man. This critical distinction is reflected in the way Jesus talks about work in the Gospels. He approaches work in two ways, as any great leader would: (1) He teaches the apostles and His followers lessons about work, and what work means to God the Father; and (2) He leads by example and shows the disciples and his followers the way He expects them to work.

JESUS CONTINUES THE WORK OF GOD ON EARTH

God describes His creation and all His deeds on Earth as work. This work is obvious to us as we observe the world around us and the universe as a whole. Included in this work is God's greatest creation, love.

God loves us so much that he sent his only son, Jesus, so that whoever believes in Him shall not perish but have eternal life. This belief is fundamental to Christianity and is essential for the Christian Capitalist to understand in the context of any business decision.

Once God incarnate, Jesus Christ, came to Earth and began His work, He clarified for those around Him that He was continuing the work that God had already started. This work was not in the form of creating additional land or oceans, and He wasn't here to create new kinds of plants or animals. Instead, He was here to tell people about God's love for them. In fact, Jesus's entire ministry can be summarized in this way: He came here to continue the work of God and spread the Good News of God's love for us. Jesus said: "My Father is still working, and I also am working" (John 5:17). Furthermore, He told everyone that the ". . . works that the Father has given me to complete, the very works that I am doing, testify on my behalf that the Father has sent me" (John 5:36).

The people of Israel in Jesus's time knew very well the story of Moses leading the ancient people of Israel out of slavery in Egypt. It must have hit home with them when He connected the dots in describing the work that God did one thousand years before and the work that Jesus was doing at that time in Israel. Jesus had just fed thousands on the shores of the Sea of Galilee, and His reputation was known throughout the region. In the following story, He scolds people for following Him just to have food. He tells the story of Moses and the people of Israel in the wilderness, how they survived only on the blessings that God gave them, and how Jesus fits into that same category. He tells the people that He is bread and doing the work that God sent Him to do. More importantly, when the people ask Him what work they need to be doing, Jesus simplifies it for them: they just need to believe in Him!

So when the crowd saw that neither Jesus nor [H]is disciples were there, they got into the boats and went to Capernaum looking for Jesus. When they found [H]im on the other side of the sea, they said to [H]im, "Rabbi, when did you come here?" Jesus answered them, "Very truly, I tell you, you are looking for me, not because you saw signs, but because you ate your fill of the loaves. Do not work for the food that perishes, but for the food that endures for eternal life, which the Son of Man will give you. For it is on [H]im that God the Father has set [H]is seal." Then they said to [H]im, "What must we do to perform the works of God?"

Jesus answered them, "This is the work of God, that you believe in [H]im whom [H]e has sent." So they said to [H]im, "What sign are you going to give us then, so that we may see it and believe you? What work are you performing? Our ancestors ate the manna in the wilderness; as it is written, 'He gave them bread from [H]eaven to eat.'" (John 6:24–31)

Jesus reminds the people that this ancient story is not the work of Moses but the work of God. By continuing the work of God on Earth, Jesus is shining a new light into the world and continues the work that God gave Him to do.

Then Jesus said to them, "Very truly, I tell you, it was not Moses who gave you the bread from [H]eaven, but it is my Father who gives you the true bread from [H]eaven. For the bread of God is that which comes down from [H]eaven and gives life to the world." They said to [H]im, "Sir, give us this bread always."

Jesus said to them, "I am the bread of life. Whoever comes to me will never be hungry, and whoever believes in me will never be thirsty. But I said to you that you have seen me and yet do not believe. Everything that the Father gives me will come to me, and anyone who comes to me I will never drive away; for I have come down from [H]eaven, not to do my own [W]ill, but the [W]ill of [H]im who sent me." (John 6:32–38)

This message was not received well by everyone. The Pharisees, a group of Jewish people in ancient Israel who followed the rules set out in the Torah very strictly, criticized Jesus heavily for claiming that He was doing God's work. The Pharisees were furious, especially after they questioned Him in the story below. When Jesus claimed that He was doing God's work and was, in fact, God, they were ready to kill Him!

At that time the festival of the Dedication took place in Jerusalem. It was winter, and Jesus was walking in the temple, in the portico of Solomon. So the Jews gathered around [H]im and said to [H]im, "How long will you keep us in suspense? If you are the Messiah, tell us plainly." Jesus answered, "I have told you, and you do not believe. The works that I do in my Father's name testify to me; but you do not believe, because you do not belong to my sheep. My sheep hear my voice. I know them, and they follow me. I give them eternal life, and they will never perish. No one will snatch them out of my hand. What my Father has given me is greater than all else, and no one can snatch it out of the Father's hand. The Father and I are one."

The Jews took up stones again to stone [H]im. Jesus replied, "I have shown you many good works from the Father. For which of these are you going to stone me?" The Jews answered, "It is not for a good work that we are going to stone you, but for blasphemy, because you, though only a human being, are making yourself God." Jesus answered, "Is it not written in your law, 'I said, you are gods'? If those to whom the [W]ord of God came were called 'gods'—and the scripture cannot be annulled—can you say that the one whom the Father has sanctified and sent into the world is blaspheming because I said, 'I am God's Son'?"

"If I am not doing the works of my Father, then do not believe me. But if I do them, even though you do not believe me, believe the works, so that you may know and understand that the Father is in me and I am in the Father." (John 10:22–38)

As we discussed earlier, people work because they are made in God's image, and the very first thing people learn about God in Holy Scripture is that God works. Jesus continues this lesson for His apostles and followers by stating that people will know that He is God because He is continuing the work of God the Father.

Even as He was performing miracles and healing people, Jesus was teaching His disciples and the people around Him about the nature of His work as arising from God's love for us.

As [H]e walked along, [H]e saw a man blind from birth. His disciples asked [H]im, "Rabbi, who sinned, this man or his parents, that he was born blind?" Jesus answered, "Neither this man nor his parents sinned; he was born blind so that God's works might be revealed in him. We must work the works of [H]im who sent me while it is day; night is coming when no one can work. As long as I am in the world, I am the light of the world." (John 9:1–5)

As the light of the world, Jesus brought God's love to all who accept Him as the Savior. In this role, we are thus part of the body of Christ and in a closer relationship with God. For the Christian Capitalist, therefore, the circle is complete: while doing work in the name of Jesus, we are in the light and become one with Him in God's name.

In the end, even as Jesus was preparing for His death on the cross, to save us all from sin, He prayed to God and glorified God through His work here on Earth: "I glorified you on Earth by finishing the work that you gave me to do" (John 17:4). Thus, Christian Capitalists understand that the work they do both comes from God and glorifies Him.

The lesson is straightforward. Jesus tells us that if people work as He has worked and follow Him as the light of the world, their work is not only going to glorify God, but it is done in God. The Christian Capitalist, therefore, hears this lesson and glorifies God through work just as Jesus did: "And this is the judgment, that the light has come into the world, and people loved darkness rather than light because their deeds were evil. For all who do evil hate the light and do not come to the light, so that their deeds may not be exposed. But those who do what is true come to the light, so that it may be clearly seen that **their deeds have been done in God**" (John 3:19–21, emphasis added).

ASK AND YOU SHALL RECEIVE

Just as Jesus tells the apostles and followers that their primary work is to believe in Him, He likewise tells them that they really only have to do one thing to achieve their goals. Jesus was here on Earth to perform the work that God sent Him to do. When the Apostle Philip asked Him to show everyone the Father,

Jesus said to him, "Have I been with you all this time, Philip, and you still do not know me? Whoever has seen me has seen the Father. How can you say, 'Show us the Father'?

Do you not believe that I am in the Father and the Father is in me? The words that I say to you I do not speak on my own; but the Father who dwells in me does [H]is works. Believe me that I am in the Father and the Father is in me; but if you do not, then believe me because of the works themselves. Very truly, I tell you, the one who believes in me will also do the works that I do and, in fact, will do greater works than these, because I am going to the Father. I will do whatever you ask in my name, so that the Father may be glorified in the Son. If in my name you ask me for anything, I will do it." (John 14:9–14)

The Christian Capitalist has two ways to consider these lessons from the Gospels: (1) they are an opportunity to use prayer to seek God's guidance in business ventures, and (2) they are directed to live generously and help others through the blessings that God shares with them as a result.

For two thousand years, Christians have pondered the meaning of Matthew's Gospel lesson and what it means to seek and find. In very simple terms, Jesus tells everyone that if they ask, God will grant their prayerful requests. The problem is that God answers prayers and provides things to us based on what He determines people need, not on what they think they need. For example, if everyone prayed to win the lottery every day, there would be no functioning lottery, and no one would work to keep the world functioning! Instead, God grants prayer requests based on what He knows is best for His children.

The Christian Capitalist understands this and prays for guidance for business ventures, both large and small. Whether it relates to a management decision, a job change, or even starting a new business, Jesus tells everyone that it is critical to seek the will of God in everything we do.

> *Ask, and it will be given you; search, and you will find; knock, and the door will be opened for you. For everyone who asks receives, and everyone who searches finds, and for everyone who knocks, the door will be opened.*
>
> *Is there anyone among you who, if your child asks for bread, will give a stone? Or if the child asks for a fish, will give a snake?*
>
> *If you then, who are evil, know how to give good gifts to your children, how much more will your Father in heaven give good things to those who ask [H]im! (Matthew 7:7–11)*

Jesus isn't just talking about requesting blessings from God for personal needs or benefits. In that ancient economy, in which so many people lived "hand to mouth," the poverty was extreme by today's standards. In that context, Jesus tells the apostles and His followers that the blessings that flow from God's answers to prayers have to be shared with others: "In everything do to others as you would have them do to you; for this is the law and the prophets" (Matthew 7:12). Luke tells the "knock, and the door will be opened" story but takes the same lesson one step further and summarizes: "If you then, who are evil, know how to give good gifts to your children, how much more will the [H]eavenly Father give the Holy Spirit to those who ask [H]im!" (Luke 11:13; see also Mark 11:22–25).

JESUS USES WORK TO TEACH ABOUT THE KINGDOM OF HEAVEN

One of the most famous parables that Jesus uses to teach the people about God's grace in the Kingdom of Heaven is the parable of the workers in the vineyard. Jesus said:

> *For the [K]ingdom of [H]eaven is like a landowner who went out early in the morning to hire laborers for his vineyard. After agreeing with the laborers for the usual daily wage, he sent them into his vineyard. When he went out about nine o'clock, he saw others standing idle in the marketplace; and he said to them, "You also go into the vineyard, and I will pay you whatever is right." So they went. When he went out again about noon and about three o'clock, he did the same. And about five o'clock he went out and found others standing around; and he said to them, "Why are you standing here idle all day?" They said to him, "Because no one has hired us." He said to them, "You also go into the vineyard."*

> *When evening came, the owner of the vineyard said to his manager, "Call the laborers and give them their pay, beginning with the last and then going to the first." When those hired about five o'clock came, each of them received the usual daily wage. Now when the first came, they thought they would receive more; but each of them also received the usual daily wage. And when they received it, they grumbled against the landowner, saying, "These last worked only one hour, and you have made them equal to us who have borne the burden of the day and the scorching heat."*

*But he replied to one of them, "Friend, I am doing you
no wrong; did you not agree with me for the usual daily
wage? Take what belongs to you and go; I choose to give
to this last the same as I give to you. Am I not allowed
to do what I choose with what belongs to me? Or are
you envious because I am generous?"* **So the last will be
first, and the first will be last.** *(Matthew 20:1–16,
emphasis added)*

Jesus Christ is a teacher, a prophet, a healer, a leader, and ultimately the founder of the Church on Earth. As Paul says in
his letter to the Colossians, He is the firstborn of all creation
and the head of the Church. He is not, however, a manager,
a business owner, or a human resources expert in the twenty-
first century! As a result, it is important to put the first parable
about work in the Kingdom of Heaven in perspective. Jesus
does not tell his followers about the workers in the vineyard
because He is starting a new trend in economics. He doesn't
tell this parable to His followers because they are trying to
develop a new model of productivity. Most of all, He doesn't
share this parable with His followers with any kind of economic message in mind. Instead, the message from the Gospel
of Matthew is one about God's love for His children and the
wide-open door to the Kingdom of Heaven!

While Jesus is a rebel in many senses of the word, especially in overturning the temple culture in ancient Israel,
His lesson about the workers in the vineyard has nothing to
do with economics or incentivizing productivity in workers.
Instead, He uses work in the vineyard as an analogy to show
that the Kingdom of Heaven is available to all, regardless of
when they invite Jesus into their heart and accept God and
His commandments. Why use this parable? In the agricultural
economy of that time, everyone understood the burden of a
hard day's work in the vineyard and how the backbreaking

toil could ultimately impact a person over the years. To have a latecomer, especially after a hard day, be paid the same as his coworkers would have been a surprise and probably anger most of the coworkers.

Nevertheless, Jesus isn't teaching a lesson on economics, and He isn't trying to teach us, as we would say in modern terms, about the "recruitment and retention" of the workers in the field. Given the sentiments of many Americans today, people who see other workers making just as much for working one hour as working a full day would absolutely work only the one hour if that was all that was required! Instead, Jesus tells this story to His apostles and followers to encourage them to go forth and spread the Good News around the world that God's salvation is open to all who accept Him, whenever they accept Him.

While Jesus tells the story of the workers in the vineyard to let everyone know God's love is available and open to all, He is also providing a warning to everyone to get along with their efforts to accept God or risk the consequences. In the parable of the withered fig tree, Jesus shows His apostles and followers that they must be productive at doing God's will or risk the wrath of God.

> *In the morning, when [H]e returned to the city, [H]e was hungry. And seeing a fig tree by the side of the road, [H]e went to it and found nothing at all on it but leaves. Then [H]e said to it, "May no fruit ever come from you again!" And the fig tree withered at once. When the disciples saw it, they were amazed, saying, "How did the fig tree wither at once?" Jesus answered them, "Truly I tell you, if you have faith and do not doubt, not only will you do what has been done to the fig tree, but even if you say to this mountain, 'Be lifted up and thrown into the sea,' it will be done.*

Whatever you ask for in prayer with faith, you will receive." (Matthew 21:18–22)

To modern ears, this parable of the withered fig tree has a sound of fire and brimstone to it. To the Christian Capitalist, however, the message is more optimistic. Instead of coming across as a threat, Jesus's parable of the withered fig tree is a message of strength in faith. Jesus curses the fig tree so that it won't bear fruit again because it has not produced fruit as God intended. That is not the end of the message, however, as Jesus uses His curse on the fig tree as a model for His disciples. If they carry even a portion of the faith that He uses to wither the fig tree, they can move mountains. For Christian Capitalists who embrace their faith and get about doing the work of God, their faith can move mountains, as well!

In teaching about the Kingdom of Heaven, Jesus uses yet another work analogy that everyone in an agrarian economy would understand: one sows and another one reaps.

Jesus said to them, "My food is to do the will of [H]im who sent me and to complete [H]is work. Do you not say, 'Four months more, then comes the harvest'? But I tell you, look around you, and see how the fields are ripe for harvesting. The reaper is already receiving wages and is gathering fruit for eternal life, so that sower and reaper may rejoice together. For here the saying holds true, 'One sows and another reaps.' I sent you to reap that for which you did not labor. Others have labored, and you have entered into their labor." (John 4:34–38)

Because He was teaching His lessons to people in an agricultural environment, Jesus used yet another analogy involving work in the Kingdom of Heaven. In this parable, Jesus reminds His apostles that He is continuing God's work by "reaping" souls on Earth and bringing them into the Kingdom of Heaven.

In addition to talking about the vineyard and the workers, he also compared the Kingdom of Heaven to a garden and God to a gardener:

> *Then [H]he told this parable: "A man had a fig tree planted in his vineyard; and he came looking for fruit on it and found none. So he said to the gardener, 'See here! For three years I have come looking for fruit on this fig tree, and still I find none. Cut it down! Why should it be wasting the soil?' He replied, 'Sir, let it alone for one more year, until I dig around it and put manure on it. If it bears fruit next year, well and good; but if not, you can cut it down.'" (Luke 13:6–9)*

Just as He cursed the unproductive fig tree, here Jesus uses a parable of work to show God's mercy for all. Instead of allowing the owner of the vineyard to cut down the tree, the gardener pleads for salvation for the tree. The landowner relents and allows the gardener additional time to help the tree become productive. The implication for Jesus's ministry is clear: God has sent Him here to do His work, and He will save those who repent and follow Jesus. The message for those who do not follow Jesus is also clear, as the landowner only allows the gardener an additional year to make the tree productive. If it is not, then it will be cut down!

JESUS TEACHES THE PEOPLE TO WORK

Jesus teaches the people around Him, including His apostles and followers, that He is there to continue the work that God started. Even more so, He teaches them that He is not just a representative of God the Father. He is God made man as well. In teaching them that their primary work is simply to believe in Him as the Son of God, Jesus gives everyone a pretty simple set of instructions.

His work, however, goes much further than that. In addition to preaching the Good News that God's salvation is assured to those who believe in Him, Jesus performs miracles and individual acts of mercy to the people of Judea that guide Christian Capitalists even today. Through His work on Earth, Jesus lays a road map for work for all Christians.

The first vocation that Jesus discusses is a shepherd. Jesus takes care of His flock in a way that reflects one of the most ancient of all jobs. Today, wooden and barbed-wire fences make it difficult for us to conceive of how difficult it is to manage a herd or flock of animals. The position of shepherd requires near-constant attention and effort, especially given the prevalence of predators in more remote areas. Jesus, and all those who listened to Him in and around Judea and Jerusalem, understood this. Ultimately, a shepherd must be willing to give everything to the flock.

As the Good Shepherd, Jesus told everyone:

> The thief comes only to steal and kill and destroy. I came that they may have life, and have it abundantly. "I am the good shepherd. The good shepherd lays down his life for the sheep. The hired hand, who is not the shepherd and does not own the sheep, sees the wolf coming and leaves the sheep and runs away—and the wolf snatches them and scatters them. The hired hand runs away because a hired hand does not care for the sheep. I am the good shepherd. I know my own and my own know me, just as the Father knows me and I know the Father. And I lay down my life for the sheep. I have other sheep that do not belong to this fold. I must bring them also, and they will listen to my voice. So there will be one flock, one shepherd." (John 10:10–16)

The second vocation Jesus uses to teach people about work is the importance of being a fisherman. The first four apostles that Jesus calls into ministry are brothers Peter and Andrew and then brothers James and John. These men made their living on the Sea of Galilee by fishing and selling those fish to people in the community. While the Gospels include stories of Jesus sailing in the boats with these apostles (and occasionally walking on water next to them), Jesus only directs the men how to cast their nets: he doesn't fish Himself.

Instead, Jesus uses the fruits of their labors to feed the crowds, setting the example for modern Christians both in the abundance of His efforts and in the scale of the number of people He serves. In the dramatic story of feeding the five thousand, Jesus blends the roles of shepherd and fisherman together:

> *And they went away in the boat to a deserted place by themselves. Now many saw them going and recognized them, and they hurried there on foot from all the towns and arrived ahead of them. As [H]e went ashore, [H]e saw a great crowd; and [H]e had compassion for them, because they were like sheep without a shepherd; and [H]e began to teach them many things.*
>
> *When it grew late, [H]is disciples came to [H]im and said, "This is a deserted place, and the hour is now very late; send them away so that they may go into the surrounding country and villages and buy something for themselves to eat." But [H]e answered them, "You give them something to eat." They said to [H]im, "Are we to go and buy two hundred denarii worth of bread, and give it to them to eat?" And [H]e said to them, "How many loaves have you? Go and see." When they had found out, they said, "Five, and two fish."*
>
> *Then [H]e ordered them to get all the people to sit down in groups on the green grass. So they sat down in groups of hundreds and of fifties. Taking the five loaves and*

the two fish, [H]e looked up to [H]eaven, and blessed
and broke the loaves, and gave them to [H]is disciples
to set before the people; and [H]e divided the two fish
among them all. And all ate and were filled; and they
took up twelve baskets full of broken pieces and of the
fish. Those who had eaten the loaves numbered five
thousand men. (Mark 6:32–44)

Earlier, Jesus tells the brothers that, if they follow Him, He will
change their vocations from fishermen to fishers of people.
The Christian Capitalist is likewise called to use the fruits
of labor for the benefit of others. Unlike Jesus, the Christian
Capitalist is not likely going to serve a seafood and bread dinner to five thousand people at once! Instead, Jesus lets us know
that all things are possible through God and that the scope of
our efforts to be generous to those in need is only limited by
our own abilities, not His.

Jesus holds other vocations throughout His ministry, of
course. He teaches on a daily basis, and His apostles and followers refer to Him as "rabbi," as a result. He also heals the
sick that He encounters in His travels around Judea. To set
an example for Christian Capitalists, one final vocation that
Jesus pursues is a worker for social justice, as we would say in
modern terms.

When Jesus sees an unjust system in place based on the
temple culture of the time, He cleanses the temple and declares that it is not a marketplace:

The Passover of the Jews was near, and Jesus went up
to Jerusalem. In the temple [H]e found people selling
cattle, sheep, and doves, and the money changers seated
at their tables. Making a whip of cords, [H]e drove all
of them out of the temple, both the sheep and the cattle.
He also poured out the coins of the money changers

and overturned their tables. He told those who were selling the doves, "Take these things out of here! Stop making my Father's house a marketplace!" His disciples remembered that it was written, "Zeal for your house will consume me." (John 2:13–17)

This story has a few implications for the Christian Capitalist. First, Jesus acts decisively and forcefully to address an unjust system in His time. For two thousand years, Christians have looked to the story of the cleansing of the temple as motivation for their efforts at social justice, whatever their generation or cultural context. The Christian Capitalist can include efforts to reform unjust systems in this time as their abilities allow.

Second, from an economic perspective, Jesus separates the house of worship from the place of business. The Christian Capitalist understands that this means a church is a place for worship, for celebrating God and loving others in the name of Jesus. Instead of declaring that there should be no marketplaces, however, Jesus only declares that the house of worship is not a marketplace. Many modern churches have bookstores, coffee shops, and even counseling centers. These do not make the church a marketplace. Jesus purged the temple of those businesses that took advantage of God's people by selling them animals or items to be used in worship, or changing money, under the pretext that God required it. Christian Capitalists understand that the grace of God is available to all—free of charge!

CHRISTIANS WILL BE KNOWN BY THEIR WORKS

Jesus makes it clear that if His followers work in the way that He instructs, they will be known around the world for the work that they perform. As is so often the case, Jesus uses an analogy to teach everyone this lesson. He compares the Kingdom of Heaven to a tree, and the work performed by Christians to the fruit of that tree:

> *You will know them by their fruits. Are grapes gathered from thorns, or figs from thistles? In the same way, every good tree bears good fruit, but the bad tree bears bad fruit. A good tree cannot bear bad fruit, nor can a bad tree bear good fruit. Every tree that does not bear good fruit is cut down and thrown into the fire. (Matthew 7:16–19)*

Luke tells the same story as Matthew but with a slightly different message that rings true to the Christian Capitalist: "The good person out of the good treasure of the heart produces good, and the evil person out of evil treasure produces evil; for it is out of the abundance of the heart that the mouth speaks" (Luke 6:45). Once again, Jesus tells everyone that they will be known by the work that they perform in His name. Likewise, He indicates that real treasure has nothing to do with material possessions. Instead, the treasure of the heart is based on love of God and love of neighbor.

With this last statement of warning, Jesus tells everyone that salvation depends on a closer relationship with God and that they should follow His way. Being a "bad tree" means that a person will perish, as opposed to having eternal life with the Lord. In his Gospel, Matthew later repeats this same lesson from Jesus but adds an additional requirement: Jesus says: "Either make the tree good, and its fruit good; or make the tree bad, and its fruit bad; for the tree is known by its fruit. . . . The good person brings good things out of a good treasure, and the evil person brings evil things out of an evil treasure" (Matthew 12:33, 35).

While Jesus doesn't explain what He means by evil treasure, that phrase is reminiscent of the Psalms. In many of the Psalms from ancient times, the psalmist would complain about the rich who had gained their wealth in evil ways. This perhaps explains the connection that Jesus draws between the person and the profit. The tree (work) bears the fruit (profit).

For the Christian Capitalist, the lesson is very clear: good people use their fortune in good ways. In his Gospel, Luke takes Matthew's concept one step further. In addition to using the analogy of the good tree and the good fruit, Luke tells us that Jesus connects work to salvation:

> *No good tree bears bad fruit, nor again does a bad tree bear good fruit; for each tree is known by its own fruit. Figs are not gathered from thorns, nor are grapes picked from a bramble bush. The good person out of the good treasure of the heart produces good, and the evil person out of evil treasure produces evil;* ***for it is out of the abundance of the heart that the mouth speaks.*** *(Luke 6:43–45, emphasis added).*

Actions speak louder than words, and Jesus tells us that the good heart speaks from its abundance by producing good treasure!

The fruit of the hard work performed by Christian Capitalists is twofold: (1) successful business ownership or management includes a work environment in which all people are treated as the Christian Capitalist would like to be treated, and (2) we must generously share profits or wages with those in need.

CHAPTER 6

JESUS TEACHES US ABOUT GIVING

While the first thing we learn about God in Holy Scripture is that He works, we learn soon thereafter that He also gives. He loves us so much that He gave us His only son, Jesus, so that whoever believes in Him will have eternal life. Furthermore, God gives us everything we need to live. Jesus, as the Son of God, passes this message along to His apostles and followers throughout the Gospels.

GOD GIVES US EVERYTHING WE NEED

God provides everything that His creation requires. An important example focuses on one of the smallest, most populous birds of the air: the sparrows. Jesus discusses how God values our lives in comparison to those tiny birds. "Are not five sparrows sold for two pennies? Yet not one of them is forgotten in God's sight. But even the hairs of your head are all counted. Do not be afraid; you are of more value than many sparrows" (Luke 12:6–7). Furthermore, Jesus asks: "Are not two sparrows sold for a penny? Yet not one of them will fall to the ground apart from your Father" (Matthew 10:29).

Jesus tells everyone this story to encourage them not to worry. In times of trouble and need, God cares for all His children, just like the birds of the air.

> *Consider the ravens: they neither sow nor reap, they have neither storehouse nor barn, and yet God feeds them. Of how much more value are you than the birds! And can any of you by worrying add a single hour to your span of life? If then you are not able to do so small a thing as that, why do you worry about the rest? Consider the lilies, how they grow: they neither toil nor spin; yet I tell you, even Solomon in all his glory was not clothed like one of these. But if God so clothes the grass of the field, which is alive today and tomorrow is thrown into the oven, how much more will [H]e clothe you—you of little faith!*
>
> *And do not keep striving for what you are to eat and what you are to drink, and do not keep worrying. For it is the nations of the world that strive after all these things, and your Father knows that you need them. Instead, strive for [H]is [K]ingdom, and these things will be given to you as well. Do not be afraid, little flock, for it is your Father's good pleasure to give you the [K]ingdom."*
> *(Luke 12:24–32; see also Matthew 6:25–34)*

Jesus encourages His followers not to worry, and He points to both the birds of the air and the lilies of the field as examples of how God cares for and tends to His creation. Instead of material considerations, Jesus implores everyone to think of the Kingdom of Heaven. As the great hymn later echoes, Jesus tells everyone: "seek ye first the Kingdom of God"! Jesus reiterates this to His followers:

> *Therefore do not worry, saying, "What will we eat?" or "What will we drink?" or "What will we wear?" For it is the Gentiles who strive for all these things; and indeed your heavenly Father knows that you need all these things. But strive first for the [K]ingdom of God and [H]is righteousness, and all these things will be given to you as well." (Matthew 6:31–33).*

One of the most satisfied and devout Christians that I have ever met was a homeless man living in a big city park. My friend, Peter, and I had set out into this park, which was known to be frequented by homeless people. In our affluent and predetermined mindset, Peter and I thought that we would bring food filled with protein down to this park and distribute it to the homeless as needed. Our goal was to visit with as many people as we could to understand more about their situation and how we, as representatives of the Church, could assist them. Once we met our new friend, we quickly learned that he had a lot to teach us!

The park had a number of trees, benches, and rolling hills, which made it easy for people without any furniture or belongings to sit and rest. It was fairly large in size, so when Peter and I arrived, we found three or four dozen homeless folks all around various parts of the park. When we approached George, he smiled broadly and greeted us. It was a warm spring day, but George was wearing an overcoat, hat, and gloves as if he was ready for the chill of the evening.

We visited with him for a few minutes and then asked him if he needed any food. George grinned again, revealing a smile with only a partial set of teeth. "No thanks, fellas, I've got enough food already." He opened his bag, which was basically a rectangular soft-sided cooler with a carrying strap. To our surprise, Peter and I saw immediately why George refused our offer of a few boiled eggs and peanut butter sandwiches: his bag was filled with sandwiches in clear plastic bags. With a quick glance, I counted nearly thirty of them!

George patted the bag. "God gives me everything I need. I've got this food, I have a beautiful place to live in this park, and I have friends here. At night, when it gets cold, or when it rains, I go stay under that bridge." He pointed toward the interstate a couple hundred yards away. "I pray to God every day, and he provides me with exactly what I need, when I need it. I've never gone hungry, I've never been hurt, and I have a happy life here in the park. God takes care of me, and I thank Him for it."

Peter and I looked at each other in amazement. We couldn't believe what George was saying. We'd come to this park thinking that every homeless person there would be desperate for food and the assistance that we could provide. We assumed that they would be anxious to live in a house like we had, eat fancy food like we did, and enjoy all the trappings of life that can come with money. Instead, George completely disrupted our preconceived notions of what homelessness is like. More importantly, he echoed exactly what Jesus told his apostles and followers two thousand years ago: God will take care of you, so don't worry!

George finished our lesson on giving and gratitude by simply saying, "I appreciate y'all offering to give me those sandwiches and boiled eggs, but I really feel like someone else could use them more than me." Peter and I just shook our heads, amazed at our own conceited assumptions. George taught us a lesson on faith that far surpassed anything we could've learned in seminary!

When Jesus tells His apostles and followers that God will take care of them, just like He does the birds of the air and the lillies of the field, He does so in a way that reminds us that only God understands what we need, when, and where.

As is so often the case, the message for the Christian Capitalist is twofold. First, the comparison of the value of a human life to a bird or plant gives encouragement to the Christian Capitalist. Whether working as a corporate executive, a small business owner, or an employee of any of these kinds of businesses, the Christian Capitalist understands that even in times in which a business is not doing well, God will provide for both Christian Capitalists and their families. Second, the Christian Capitalist recognizes that in this modern world, food, clothing, housing, and financial assistance don't rain down on people like manna from heaven. These things have to be provided, and Christian Capitalists are the providers. Christian Capitalists are here to do the work of God on His behalf and care for those in need.

As Jesus commissions His disciples and sends them around Judea and the Sea of Galilee to spread the Good News, He specifically instructs them not to take anything. This shows us that relying on the generosity of others has always been a part of people's relationship with God through His son, Jesus.

> *After this the Lord appointed seventy others and sent them ahead of [H]im in pairs to every town and place where [H]e [H]imself intended to go. He said to them, "The harvest is plentiful, but the laborers are few; therefore ask the Lord of the harvest to send out laborers into [H]is harvest. Go on your way. See, I am sending you out like lambs into the midst of wolves. Carry no purse, no bag, no sandals; and greet no one on the road. Whatever house you enter, first say, 'Peace to this house!' And if anyone is there who shares in peace, your peace will rest on that person; but if not, it will return to you. Remain in the same house, eating and drinking whatever*

they provide, for the laborer deserves to be paid. Do not move about from house to house. Whenever you enter a town and its people welcome you, eat what is set before you; cure the sick who are there, and say to them, 'The [K]ingdom of God has come near to you.'

But whenever you enter a town and they do not welcome you, go out into its streets and say, 'Even the dust of your town that clings to our feet, we wipe off in protest against you. Yet know this: the [K]ingdom of God has come near.' I tell you, on that day it will be more tolerable for Sodom than for that town." (Luke 10:1–12)

Christian Capitalists understand the obligation to care for those who come to them in need. Just as Jesus's disciples would come to a new town and seek assistance from those residents, Christian Capitalists have to be open and available to those coming into their lives seeking assistance.

Upon their return, Jesus asks the disciples how effective it was to rely on the generosity of others as they traveled around Judea. "He said to them, 'When I sent you out without a purse, bag, or sandals, did you lack anything?' They said, 'No, not a thing'" (Luke 22:35). Just as the disciples relied on the generosity of others, Jesus instructs them to be generous in return:

These twelve Jesus sent out with the following instructions: "Go nowhere among the Gentiles, and enter no town of the Samaritans, but go rather to the lost sheep of the house of Israel. As you go, proclaim the good news, 'The [K]ingdom of [H]eaven has come near.' Cure the sick, raise the dead, cleanse the lepers, cast out demons. ***You received without payment; give without payment.*** *Take no gold, or silver, or copper in your belts, no bag for your journey, or two tunics, or sandals, or a staff;*

for laborers deserve their food." (Matthew 10:5–10, emphasis added)

Finally, Jesus directly connects giving and receiving by letting His followers know that giving to others is the key to being part of the body of Christ: "Very truly, I tell you, whoever receives one whom I send receives me; and whoever receives me receives [H]im who sent me" (John 13:20).

JESUS PROVIDES ROLE MODELS FOR GIVING

As we have discussed previously in this book, Jesus regularly used parables, or fictional stories with a purpose, to teach His apostles and followers. He would also take advantage of the traveling nature of His ministry and make note of the learning opportunities that everyone saw as they traveled around Judea. In fact, one of the greatest parables that Jesus told that reverberates two thousand years later is based on a traveler who got in trouble and was left for dead. In this section, we explore three role models for giving provided by Jesus.

The Widow's Mite: Give Until It Hurts!

As Jesus and His disciples sit in the temple during a break from their travels, He takes time to point out a widow who was putting coins (mites) into the treasury.

> *He sat down opposite the treasury, and watched the crowd putting money into the treasury. Many rich people put in large sums. A poor widow came and put in two small copper coins, which are worth a penny. Then [H]e called his disciples and said to them, "Truly I tell you, this poor widow has put in more than all those who are contributing to the treasury. For all of them have*

contributed out of their abundance; but she out of her poverty has put in everything she had, all she had to live on." (Mark 12:41–44; see also Luke 21:1–4)

The implications of the widow's mite story are twofold for the Christian Capitalist. The first underscores one of the themes of this book itself. Anyone can be a Christian Capitalist, regardless of how they participate in the economy, and what their role is in a particular business. For the small business owner, Fortune 500 executive, entry-level employee, or retiree, the Christian Capitalist Ethic is simple: the more we make, the more we give.

This lesson from the widow's mite story reveals that giving is relative. Jesus notes that the rich people are giving according to their means, but He is more impressed by the widow who gave everything she had. Two thousand years later, the message for the Christian Capitalist is clear: you can make minimum wage, be a retiree living on a pension, or be a millionaire; it doesn't matter to Jesus. His message is that we should all give as much as we can when we can.

Second, the context behind the story of the widow's mite is that in Jesus's time, rich people were held in high esteem and were expected to give more. Poor people, however, were looked down upon and possibly thought of as less-valuable members of society. Sounds familiar to modern ears! That is most certainly the case in our modern world. It must have been shocking for the disciples, therefore, to hear Jesus praise a widow who gave only two small coins worth a penny above the rich people who gave far more extravagant sums.

This story of the widow often reminds me of the church on my college campus, a beautiful Gothic cathedral with towering arches and a gigantic pipe organ that rivals many of the great cathedrals of Europe. On a sunny day, the stained glass would light up the interior of the church and make it shine brightly with a kaleidoscope of colors.

For two years, I volunteered as an usher at that church and greatly enjoyed that ministry. No matter what kind of hijinks I had gotten myself into the Saturday night before, I would manage to get cleaned up and make my way to the church in time for the main service on Sunday morning. This church was so formal that all the members of the congregation wore suits and fancy dresses, and the children were decked out in their finery. One of my favorite parts of the experience was that I did not need to get dressed up in a coat and tie because ushers at this church wore bright blue robes!

Typically wearing shorts and a T-shirt, I would go through the back door of the church, don my blue robe, and emerge at the front door with stacks of bulletins to distribute to the faithful.

Once the members of the congregation were in the pews, I would retire to a side area in the church and wait for the next big role: passing the offering plates!

At the appropriate time in the worship service, the pastor would announce that it was time for the offertory. Six of us would grab two plates apiece and then proceed down the middle of the aisle of this giant church and pass the plates down the pews. Although all the ushers were between eighteen and twenty-two years old, and the vast majority of the members of the congregation were families from our community, not college students, we felt empowered by the blue robes and our roles as ushers. As we passed the offering plates, we would exhort the members of the congregation by whispering: "Give till it hurts!"

In hindsight, I suppose we felt comfortable taking this aggressive position with the members of the congregation because we didn't have any money and we recognized that they did. It may have also simply been because we thought needling these good folks was funny. Either way, it taught me an important lesson: the widow and her two coins provide an example for Christians that echoes through the ages!

The Good Samaritan

When discussing the concept of giving in relation to the Bible, it's imperative that we explore the context and message of the famous Good Samaritan parable. The dispute between the people of Israel and the people of Samaria went back a couple of centuries before Jesus's time. It was based on disagreements of Holy Scripture and politics. The big thing to know about the relationship between those two groups of people is that the people of Israel despised the Samaritans.

The Samaritans were ostracized from Hebrew society, and faithful Jews would not have considered a Samaritan as anything other than a detestable enemy. With that in mind, note the traditional roles of the characters that the people of Israel typically held in high esteem. Both were undermined and criticized by Jesus as he tells the story of the Good Samaritan.

Just then a lawyer stood up to test Jesus. "Teacher," he said, "what must I do to inherit eternal life?" He said to him, "What is written in the law? What do you read there?" He answered, "You shall love the Lord your God with all your heart, and with all your soul, and with all your strength, and with all your mind; and your neighbor as yourself." And [H]e said to him, "You have given the right answer; do this, and you will live." But wanting to justify himself, he asked Jesus, "And who is my neighbor?"

Jesus replied, "A man was going down from Jerusalem to Jericho, and fell into the hands of robbers, who stripped him, beat him, and went away, leaving him half dead. Now by chance a priest was going down that road; and

*when he saw him, he passed by on the other side. So
likewise a Levite, when he came to the place and saw
him, passed by on the other side.*

*But a Samaritan while traveling came near him; and
when he saw him, he was moved with pity. He went to
him and bandaged his wounds, having poured oil and
wine on them. Then he put him on his own animal,
brought him to an inn, and took care of him. The next
day he took out two denarii, gave them to the innkeeper,
and said, 'Take care of him; and when I come back, I
will repay you whatever more you spend.' Which of these
three, do you think, was a neighbor to the man who
fell into the hands of the robbers?" He said, "The one
who showed him mercy." Jesus said to him, "**Go and do
likewise.**" (Luke 10:25–37, emphasis added)*

Today, hundreds of hospitals and health care organizations are
named after the story of the Good Samaritan because they provide care to those in need without regard to their ability to pay.
These Good Samaritan health care providers are terrific examples of Christian Capitalists coming to work together to take
care of the poor, the needy, and the sick in their communities.
The lasting impact of this parable, therefore, is significant.

The Christian Capitalist looks at these Good Samaritan
organizations and notes two things. First, the tradition of assisting others in the name of mercy is exactly what Jesus has in
mind for modern Christians when he tells the smart-mouthed
lawyer to go and do likewise! Second, and more importantly,
the Good Samaritan goes over and above simple financial
assistance by taking care of the victim in the story by cleaning
him up, treating his wounds, and carrying him to the inn.

When he gets there, the Good Samaritan doesn't just
drop the victim off at the inn but spends the night there,

taking care of the man in need and placing him in the charge of the innkeeper before heading on his way. Not only does the Good Samaritan pay for the man's stay at the inn, but he also tells the innkeeper that he will return to reimburse the innkeeper for any additional costs that he incurs when providing care to the injured man.

The implication of this is clear. Money is certainly a key part of giving for the Christian Capitalist, but a giving heart will find a way to give beyond simple financial assistance. Transportation, health care, housing, and follow-up for assisting the poor and needy are all part of the story. Therefore, the door for Christian Capitalists is wide open in terms of how we give, and the Good Samaritan provides a significant example of what that giving can entail today. Since the Christian Capitalist can be from any walk of life, and any socioeconomic background, that also means that a person reading the story who has no financial means can still have a giving heart, just like the widow who gave her two coins.

Why is all this giving so important to Jesus? He tells us the reason in the story of Zacchaeus, the tax collector.

Zaccheus the Tax Collector

The story of the widow who is praised by Jesus for giving more than the rich people in the synagogue, as well as the detestable Samaritan who outshines the efforts of the priest and the rich person, are two examples of shocking lessons within Jesus's ministry. These parables allowed Him the opportunity not only to make a point but also to ruffle some feathers.

In those times in Israel, however, no one was more reviled than tax collectors. During Jesus's life, Israel was ruled by the Roman Empire. Although a succession of Caesars had established a bureaucracy in Rome and a military presence throughout the Empire, local governors and military leaders could only do so much. Roman policy at the time was to leave religious cultures in place and recruit local officials from the ranks of the conquered to serve on behalf of the Empire in various roles. None of those roles compared to that of the tax collector.

In those days, a Jew who worked for the Roman Empire to collect extremely high taxes on behalf of Caesar (the Roman emperor who oppressed the Jews) was, simply put, a traitor. It was probably shocking to the apostles and followers of Jesus that Zacchaeus was even interested in the message that Jesus delivered wherever He went, but that is only the beginning of the story.

> He entered Jericho and was passing through it. A man was there named Zacchaeus; he was a chief tax collector and was rich. He was trying to see who Jesus was, but on account of the crowd he could not, because he was short in stature. So he ran ahead and climbed a sycamore tree to see [H]im, because [H]e was going to pass that way. When Jesus came to the place, [H]e looked up and said to him, "Zacchaeus, hurry and come down; for I must stay at your house today." So he hurried down and was happy to welcome [H]im.
>
> All who saw it began to grumble and said, "He has gone to be the guest of one who is a sinner." Zacchaeus stood there and said to the Lord, "Look, half of my possessions, Lord, I will give to the poor; and if I have defrauded anyone of anything, I will pay back four times as much." Then Jesus said to him, "Today salvation has come to this house, because he too is a son of Abraham. For the Son of Man came to seek out and to save the lost." (Luke 19:1–10)

Like the Good Samaritan, Zacchaeus plays a role that Jesus knew His apostles and followers would initially find reprehensible. Nevertheless, he has dinner with Zacchaeus and passes the Good News along to him. Zacchaeus accepts Jesus's teachings, sells half his possessions, and repays those he had deceived. Jesus grants him salvation as a result of his new faith.

The implications of this story for the Christian Capitalist are clear. First, no matter what a Christian Capitalist may have done to be at odds with the surrounding community, it is never too late to repent and act with a giving heart. Whether Christian Capitalists decide to give half of their belongings to the poor, like Zacchaeus, the simple fact is that giving is the key to this new relationship between Zacchaeus and Jesus. It could be the beginning of a new relationship between the Christian Capitalist and Jesus, too!

Second, as discussed earlier in Chapter 4 on the Kingdom of Heaven, Jesus succinctly and quietly provides that the keys to the Kingdom can be earned by giving generously. Zaccheus has earned his salvation, and the Lord grants it quickly and right there at the dinner table! Although Luke doesn't tell us what happens to Zaccheus after dinner that night, the Christian Capitalist knows that his life is changed forever in just the course of a few minutes through generous giving. The Christian Capitalist, therefore, searches to take those opportunities whenever, wherever, and however, they present themselves!

GIVING IS A WINDOW TO THE HEART: SERVING GOD WITH WEALTH

One of the themes of Holy Scripture is that material possessions and wealth can interfere with a person's relationship with God. Jesus, in particular, teaches us a lot about having a closer relationship with God and not letting wealth interfere. In this complex relationship of how our spiritual and financial lives are intertwined, Christian Capitalists have to balance two distinct concepts. First, following Jesus as the way, the truth, and the life is a means of discipleship and worshiping God. Second, disciples following the path of Jesus have to make sense of Jesus's direction that we cannot serve God and wealth at the same time.

Jesus Tells Everyone to Pick Up Your Cross and Follow Him

Jesus puts the priority of God over wealth and His ministry over material possessions into physical terms that all His apostles and followers can understand: you can't hold the cross while you're holding a bag of money!

> *He called the crowd with [H]is disciples, and said to them, "If any want to become my followers, let them deny themselves and take up their cross and follow me. For those who want to save their life will lose it, and those who lose their life for my sake, and for the sake of the [G]ospel, will save it. For what will it profit them to gain the whole world and forfeit their life? Indeed, what can they give in return for their life?" (Mark 8:34–37)*

While it is impossible for a person to pick up the cross when his or her hands are full of possessions, Jesus certainly leaves open the option to serve God through wealth. Over the last two thousand years, Christian Capitalists have followed this path. Jesus says: "Whoever does not carry the cross and follow me cannot be my disciple. . . . So therefore, none of you can become my disciple if you do not give up all your possessions" (Luke 14:27, 33).

While working hard to earn more, Jesus wants His followers to share generously with those in need within their communities.

> *As [H]e was setting out on a journey, a man ran up and knelt before [H]im, and asked [H]im, "Good Teacher,*

what must I do to inherit eternal life?" Jesus said to him, "Why do you call me good?" No one is good but God alone. You know the commandments: 'You shall not murder; You shall not commit adultery; You shall not steal; You shall not bear false witness; You shall not defraud; Honor your father and mother.'" He said to [H]im, "Teacher, I have kept all these since my youth."

*Jesus, looking at him, loved him and said, "You lack one thing; go, sell what you own, and give the money to the poor, and you will have **treasure in [H]eaven**; then come, follow me." When he heard this, he was shocked and went away grieving, for he had many possessions. (Mark 10:17–22, emphasis added)*

These are questions that have arisen ever since Jesus preached His message two thousand years ago. Giving to the poor is the key to finding treasure in Heaven. In a similar version of the story in the Gospel of Matthew, "Jesus said to him, 'If you wish to be perfect, go, sell your possessions, and give the money to the poor, and you will have **treasure in [H]eaven**; then come, follow me.' When the young man heard this word, he went away grieving, for he had many possessions" (Matthew 19:21–22, emphasis added).

In very plain terms, Jesus tells His followers that they can find treasure in Heaven through sharing their treasure on Earth: "Sell your possessions, and give alms. Make purses for yourselves that do not wear out, an unfailing **treasure in [H]eaven**, where no thief comes near and no moth destroys. **For where your treasure is, there your heart will be als**o" (Luke 12:33–34, emphasis added; see also Mark 6:21).

For the Christian Capitalist, these are some of the most challenging verses in all the Scriptures. So how does the Christian Capitalist comply with Jesus's directive to give away all his possessions? Jesus doesn't tell us exactly how to go about doing this. Who gets our possessions? How? When?

Furthermore, this directive may put people at odds with the great Second Commandment that Jesus gives us: love your neighbor as yourself. If someone gives all their possessions away, that person then must rely on the generosity of others to survive and becomes a potential burden to their neighbor. Is that any way to love them?

Although Jesus uses a strong example to make His point in these verses, He ultimately puts Christian Capitalists on notice that their material possessions interfere with their faith in Him! This is challenging for the Christian Capitalist, as the inherent nature of capitalism is to generate wealth. While Jesus is certainly clear in His message that God must come first, the Christian Capitalist can take the message and interpret it as an additional command: **we cannot serve God and wealth, but we can serve God with our wealth!**

When Jesus tells the crowd that "none of you can become my disciple if you do not give up all your possessions," he puts accumulating material possessions and following the path of Jesus squarely at odds! How can one make sense of these principles?

Becoming a disciple of Jesus means putting God first and foremost—above all, people and things. Luke mentions that Jesus goes so far as to tell people that they should forsake their family members and only love God. Simply put, Jesus tells us that you cannot pick up the cross if your hands are full of possessions. Such possessions interfere with a person's relationship with God.

On the flip side of the proverbial coin, we know that Jesus owned possessions, just like His contemporaries and modern people. Because tradition holds that He was a carpenter, we can conclude that He probably had tools for His trade.

We know that He had sandals because Mary Magdalene removed them to put oil on His feet. We know He had at least one robe because the soldiers took it from Him on Good Friday. So, while owning some possessions is a necessity in life, those possessions shouldn't interfere with our relationship with God.

Serving God with Our Wealth

Picking up the cross, of course, is a metaphor. People come to the cross with their hearts and minds, not literally with their hands and feet. When Jesus tells everyone that they have to give up all their possessions, He is telling everyone to free their hearts and minds of anything, or anyone, that could take them from the path that God sets before them. His followers need to free themselves from distractions in following the way to the treasure in Heaven.

Jesus repeatedly tells His apostles and followers that a person can't serve God and wealth. What does He mean by this? People have debated this for millennia. In one explanation, Jesus may mean that a person has to put God before money every time. Another interpretation is that a person can only be a Christian if he or she is poor. Many monks and nuns, as well as clergy, over the years have taken vows of poverty in deference to this principle.

For the Christian Capitalist, however, Jesus's position is a challenge. By telling everyone that a person can't serve both God and wealth, Jesus tells Christian Capitalists that they can serve God's allegiance by focusing solely on God first. Jesus tells us that wealth must always come second:

> *Do not store up for yourselves treasures on Earth, where moth and rust consume and where thieves break in and steal; but store up for yourselves treasures in [H]eaven, where neither moth nor rust consumes and where thieves do not break in and steal.* ***For where your treasure***

is, there your heart will be also. (Matthew 6:19–21, emphasis added)

When Jesus instructs us that we cannot serve two masters, He's talking about putting God first, over and above all else. He makes it clear that people cannot serve God and wealth. In the Sermon on the Mount in the Gospel of Matthew, He puts it bluntly: "No one can serve two masters; for a slave will either hate the one and love the other, or be devoted to the one and despise the other. **You cannot serve God and wealth**" (Matthew 6:24, emphasis added).

As part of the parable of the dishonest manager, Luke tells the story in a different way than Matthew, with the same ultimate message regarding God's priority over wealth. Jesus said:

> *"Whoever is faithful in a very little is faithful also in much; and whoever is dishonest in a very little is dishonest also in much. If then you have not been faithful with the dishonest wealth, who will entrust to you the true riches? And if you have not been faithful with what belongs to another, who will give you what is your own? No slave can serve two masters; for a slave will either hate the one and love the other, or be devoted to the one and despise the other. **You cannot serve God and wealth.**" The Pharisees, who were lovers of money, heard all this, and they ridiculed [H]im.* (Luke 16:10–14, emphasis added)

Jesus's message to His followers that they can't serve God and wealth goes hand in hand with His admonition to His apostles that everyone should sell all their possessions to pick up the cross and follow Him. The two concepts flow to the same ultimate point: discipleship and worship of God must come before everything else in the Earthly kingdom in order to be best prepared for the Kingdom of Heaven.

Give That Which Is Within

One of the themes of Jesus's teaching is that actions, not words, show what is in a person's heart. Much more so than following the rules that the Pharisees clung to so desperately, Jesus emphasizes what people did to serve God rather than the written law of their ancestors.

Jesus tells the Pharisees that what matters is within, and they should give that which is within as charity.

> *While [H]e was speaking, a Pharisee invited [H]im to dine with him; so [H]e went in and took [H]is place at the table. The Pharisee was amazed to see that [H]e did not first wash before dinner. Then the Lord said to him, "Now you Pharisees clean the outside of the cup and of the dish, but inside you are full of greed and wickedness. You fools! Did not the one who made the outside make the inside also?* **So give for alms those things that are within***; and see, everything will be clean for you." (Luke 11:37–41, emphasis added)*

Here, Jesus makes that connection complete by saying that it doesn't matter if someone eats supper with dirty hands, since it all comes from God. Furthermore, when He tells the Pharisee to give alms from within, Christian Capitalists understand that Jesus is telling His apostles and followers that they must give to the poor and the needy as their hearts guide them.

While the bulk of this book focuses on giving in a financial sense, giving comes from within and therefore includes giving of time and talent. Whatever a Christian Capitalist can give, it must come from within! When Jesus tells everyone to make everything clean, He's not speaking in a literal sense. He means that God makes all things new in the Kingdom of Heaven, which everyone can enter by doing His Will. In addition, the message of "giving comes from within" follows the message from the story of the widow's mite. Giving alms from within not only lets Christian Capitalists know that they must give generously but that the amount is relative.

My friend told me a story recently about giving that underscores the point that we are only stewards of the blessings that God gives us. Linda was a hardworking executive for a big company, and she handled the financial affairs for the company very well. The CEO of the company gave her a Christmas present, which was simply a Christmas card with a $100 bill included. What a generous way to celebrate Christmas! Linda thanked him profusely and told him that she really appreciated the gesture, although it certainly wasn't necessary. She had a strong work ethic and sense of duty.

On the way home from another hard day at work, she stopped off at a restaurant that had a drive-through window to pick up supper for her family. She pulled her car into the driveway and moved up next to the speaker to place her order. "Welcome," a friendly voice said. "May I take your order?" Linda replied with the order for her family's meal. When the attendant from the restaurant told her the amount that was due and asked her to drive around to the pickup window, he followed with: "Thank you for coming to our restaurant today. We are glad you're here, and I can't wait to see you at the pickup window!"

Linda had had a hard day, and hearing that energetic, welcoming voice, put a broad smile on her face. In fact, she would later reflect that it made her whole day! As a Christian Capitalist, she knew what she had to do. As she pulled up to the pickup window, the attendant smiled and said:

"Good evening! Thank you again for coming to our restaurant." Then he told her how much she had to pay for the meal.

Linda responded by thanking him, handing over her credit card for payment, and asking to see the manager. The attendant's face changed immediately. "Is there something wrong, ma'am?" Linda replied: "Quite the opposite! May I please speak to your manager?" The attendant went to get the manager on duty, and with a big smile on her face, Linda told the manager: "I've had a really hard day, but just hearing this man's voice, his positive energy, and welcoming attitude over the speaker made my whole day. I wanted you to be here when I gave him this gift." She then turned to the seat next to her, grabbed the card that she had received earlier in the day, pulled out the $100 bill, and handed it to the attendant. "Here, please take this. You deserve it more than me."

He was so overwhelmed with surprise and joy that tears began streaming down his cheeks! Even as she was telling me the story, Linda got teary-eyed herself! Like any Christian Capitalist, she understood that there are rare opportunities in life to bring true joy to someone through a complete surprise. She felt that **she was blessed with the opportunity to give in that moment**.

Hard work is hardwired in all of us, and Linda certainly deserved the bonus that she had received from the CEO of her company. Nevertheless, giving is likewise a part of who we are as humans. Linda took the opportunity to share the blessing she had received with someone else, and instead of feeling any sense of obligation or hesitation, she gave freely and with joy because she was called by God to do so. Like Linda, the Christian Capitalist looks for opportunities to share the blessings that God has provided and experience that joy of giving.

The Rich Man and Lazarus— The Giving Imperative

For the bulk of Holy Scripture, and this book, the focus on giving to the needy is on the benefits that derive to both the giver and the recipient. We have seen thus far that the Torah, the Psalms, and Proverbs focus on giving as part of doing God's will. In the parable of the rich man and Lazarus, however, Jesus puts a very fine point on the results of our failure to give. Jesus makes it very clear that eternal torment waits for those who walk past the needy and refuse to share the food that they have from their tables.

There was a rich man who was dressed in purple and fine linen and who feasted sumptuously every day. And at his gate lay a poor man named Lazarus, covered with sores, who longed to satisfy his hunger with what fell from the rich man's table; even the dogs would come and lick his sores. The poor man died and was carried away by the angels to be with Abraham. The rich man also died and was buried. In Hades, where he was being tormented, he looked up and saw Abraham far away with Lazarus by his side.

He called out, "Father Abraham, have mercy on me, and send Lazarus to dip the tip of his finger in water and cool my tongue; for I am in agony in these flames." But Abraham said, "Child, remember that during your lifetime you received your good things, and Lazarus in like manner evil things; but now he is comforted here, and you are in agony. Besides all this, between you and us a great chasm has been fixed, so that those who might want to pass from here to you cannot do so, and no one can cross from there to us."

He said, "Then, father, I beg you to send him to my father's house—for I have five brothers—that he may warn them, so that they will not also come into this place of torment." Abraham replied, "They have Moses and the prophets; they should listen to them." He said, "No, [F]ather Abraham; but if someone goes to them from the dead, they will repent." He said to him, "If they do not listen to Moses and the prophets, neither will they be convinced even if someone rises from the dead." (Luke 16:19–31)

This parable has three lessons for the Christian Capitalist.

First, Jesus tells us that the rich man had significant resources and was fully capable of assisting Lazarus. He wore purple robes and fine linen, which was the closest thing to a status symbol that ancient people had in terms of clothing. In today's language, we would say that the rich man wore designer suits and shoes.

Furthermore, the rich man's wealth was not temporary. Jesus says in the parable that he feasted sumptuously every day, so much so that Lazarus simply wanted the crumbs from the rich man's table.

Likewise, Lazarus was equally incapable of taking care of himself. Jesus doesn't describe what condition or disease crippled Lazarus, but the result is that he was not capable of working or feeding himself. Since he longed for the crumbs from the rich man's table but still was not able to get them, it is also likely that Lazarus was malnourished, probably to the point of his death. Jesus also notes that the dogs who would frequent the court would bother Lazarus by licking his sores, presumably related to whatever condition left him crippled.

The second point of this parable is that the rich man and Lazarus could have had a relationship if the rich man had followed God's will. Jesus describes the scene of Lazarus lying at the gate, presumably of the rich man's house. If Lazarus was familiar enough with the daily feast held by the rich man, then he likewise had some view into the rich man's luxurious residence, maybe even a mansion. Instead of reaching out to this poor man who dwelt at the gates of his luxurious home, the rich man passed by him day after day.

For the Christian Capitalist, this is an important moment to consider how many people he or she regularly encounters in need. Is it a man on the corner in a wheelchair with a coffee tin asking for donations? Is it coworkers who regularly complain about not having enough food for themselves or their children? Or is it someone at an intersection on the way to and from home or work? In each of these scenarios, passing by these folks on a daily basis is the equivalent of the rich man passing by Lazarus and his gate every day.

Finally, and most importantly, Jesus sends a message across two thousand years for Christian Capitalists in America: share your wealth with those in need, or else! The bulk of this parable features the rich man begging for mercy from Abraham, who holds Lazarus in his warm embrace. In this story, Abraham is a messenger from God who reiterates a message that the rich man has heard throughout his life. This message is very clear because Abraham simply reminds the rich man that he has heard from Moses and the prophets time and again that he should have shared the wealth with the poor, especially Lazarus, with whom he could easily have had a relationship.

Even when the rich man begs for his five brothers to be informed of the eventual result of this kind of selfishness and refusal to share wealth with the needy, Abraham rebukes him. If the rich man's brothers are not going to learn the message from Moses and the prophets, then they are not going to learn it at all. Both the rich man and his brothers have had plenty of opportunities, according to Abraham, to get it right.

For modern individuals striving to be Christian Capitalists, the message has a double meaning. Since Moses, the prophets, and Jesus have provided this basic guidance on what God wants people to do with their wealth, the implications are clear: share with those in need, invite them to the feast when possible, and don't ignore those who are less fortunate.

The other implication of this parable is likewise crystal clear: failure to invite others to the feast and failure to help the needy results in torment. For the Christian Capitalist, perhaps it is difficult to imagine a poor man, lying at the gate of a mansion, who is so poor and hungry that he cannot even retrieve the crumbs from the rich man's table. Instead, the Christian Capitalist looks for an opportunity to put into action the motto of the Christian Capitalists: **the more we make, the more we give!**

In an attempt to place the story of the rich man and Lazarus in today's context, I'm reminded of a time when my family and I drove to an exclusive private school in our community for a volleyball tournament. Our daughter was playing there for her school, which is also an exclusive private school. While the interstate exit is a little rough and tumble, the surrounding area is full of multimillion-dollar homes, and the vehicles that pass under this particular bridge, which carries the interstate over it, are mainly luxurious ones. Everything from the typical high-end domestic SUVs to luxury imported sedans and Italian sports cars, this underpass has hundreds, if not thousands, of wealthy people pass through it every single day.

My wife, Rebekah, was driving our car so that I could sit in the passenger seat and work on the readings for the upcoming weekend at our church, which included this parable of Lazarus. As I thought about how miserable it must be to be so hot and thirsty that you would desire relief from someone dipping their finger in water and touching it to your tongue, I finished my work and closed my laptop.

As we exited the interstate and turned to go through the underpass so that now the interstate was roaring overhead, I was surprised to see a woman standing there, smiling. The underpass had a little sidewalk, and she had managed to make her way there to stand, smile, and wave a small cardboard sign saying, "Hungry—please help." Literally within a minute or two of having just read the story of the rich man and Lazarus, God presented us with an opportunity to show that we had learned our lesson! I thought to myself, "Thank you Holy Spirit, that was fast!" and said to my wife, "I'm glad you just gave me some cash for our trip, we're going to get a chance to use it!"

A few things about this experience stood out to me. First, this woman wore a dress that appeared to be from her native country. It did not appear to be the kind of garment that one would buy in a local department store. Second, despite the clear anguish on her face from her present situation, she managed a big, beautiful smile that covered her entire face when I greeted her and gave her some money. To see her joy, even in that situation of sorrow, truly brought joy to my heart!

Third, and certainly most disturbing, was that I soon noticed she was part of a family. At the other end of the underpass stood a little girl who was a nearly identical but smaller version of her mother: same style of dress, same dark complexion and hair, and same beautiful smile! When I smiled and waved to the little girl, she smiled and waved back with a look of joy on her face that certainly belied her situation.

Surprisingly, next to the little girl was a man, presumably the father and husband of this little family. He was taller, slim, and athletic-looking and wore a beard and a soccer jersey. This further underscored my initial impression that these folks were visiting from another country and could possibly explain why they managed to find themselves under an interstate bridge. Finally, and heartbreakingly, the man was tending to a baby in a stroller.

As Christian Capitalists contemplate the parable of the rich man and Lazarus, they must ask how this parable fits into their lives today. Merely understanding the importance of giving and compassion is not enough to satisfy the call of all Christians. The act of giving is the takeaway from this story. While I certainly didn't do all that the Good Samaritan would have done, I did what was tangible for me in that moment by giving her some money. Likewise, Christian Capitalists must, very literally, reach into their wallets and change a circumstance from heartbreaking to joy to the best of their abilities.

The Golden Rule

Jesus's primary message is that the Kingdom of Heaven is available to all people through God's love. In the Sermon on the Mount, He tells the poor and needy, who surround Him on the mountain, that the poor, sorrowful, meek, and hungry will all be blessed as a result of the Kingdom of Heaven coming to Earth. This blessing comes with a fresh perspective. Jesus reiterates all the laws of the Torah and the messages of the prophets into two main commandments: love God above all else and love your neighbor as yourself.

> *When the Pharisees heard that [H]e had silenced the Sadducees, they gathered together, and one of them, a lawyer, asked [H]im a question to test [H]im. "Teacher, which commandment in the law is the greatest?" He said to him, "'You shall love the Lord your God with all your heart, and with all your soul, and with all your mind.' This is the first and greatest commandment. And a second is like it: 'You shall love your neighbor as yourself.' On these two commandments hang all the law and the prophets." (Matthew 22:34–40)*

But how do we love God above all else? How do we love our neighbor as ourselves? That is the continuing message of the Gospels, and what Christians have been studying, discussing, debating, and arguing since Jesus rose into Heaven.

The Christian Capitalist Ethic, outlined in Chapter 12, is built on the twin pillars of work and giving. The two commandments, love of God and love of neighbor, are intertwined within this ethic. To love God, people must show Him love that matches His love for His children. That means working hard to meet the expectations that He has set, using the gifts that He has given people, and caring for the blessings that He provides to us. Hard work helps accomplish those goals.

Meanwhile, a person who works hard and loves God and takes the opportunity to thank God for the blessings of this life cannot accomplish both commandments of Jesus in isolation. As Jesus said, the first commandment is the love of God above all else, but the second is "like unto it." Because the commandments are equal, Christian Capitalists are obligated not only to love God above all else but to love their neighbors. This means sharing the blessings that God has given the Christian Capitalist with the people of his or her community: "Give to everyone who begs from you, and do not refuse anyone who wants to borrow from you" (Matthew 5:42).

There are certainly plenty of ways that Christians have discovered over the years to try and follow these commandments from Jesus. The Christian Capitalist, however, focuses on work and giving as the means to this end. Just as Jesus told His apostles and followers earlier about their works, giving to others is one way that people will know that the giver is a Christian: "I give you a new commandment, that you love one another. Just as I have loved you, you also should love one another. By this everyone will know that you are my disciples, if you have love for one another" (John 13:34–35). Likewise, He told everyone: "In the same way, **let your light shine before others, so that they may see your good works and give glory to your Father in [H]eaven**" (Matthew 5:16, emphasis added).

Jesus instructs the disciples on servant leadership by washing their feet on the Thursday before His crucifixion. This is a lasting and enduring image of Jesus in the role of servant leader, and it is a model for all Christian Capitalists.

So if I, your Lord and Teacher, have washed your feet, you also ought to wash one another's feet. For I have set you an example, that you also should do as I have done to you. Very truly, I tell you, servants are not greater than their master, nor are messengers greater than the one who sent them. If you know these things, you are blessed if you do them. (John 13:14–17)

Jesus tells the disciples that they help Him when they help the needy. Sometimes, people do not recognize that they are taking care of Jesus when they are taking care of others. In describing the Second Coming of the Son of Man, Jesus tells everyone that those who helped others during their lifetimes will be separated from those who didn't.

". . . for I was hungry and you gave me food, I was thirsty and you gave me something to drink, I was a stranger and you welcomed me, I was naked and you gave me clothing, I was sick and you took care of me, I was in prison and you visited me." Then the righteous will answer [H]im, "Lord, when was it that we saw you hungry and gave you food, or thirsty and gave you something to drink? And when was it that we saw you a stranger and welcomed you, or naked and gave you clothing? And when was it that we saw you sick or in prison and visited you?" And the [K]ing will answer them, "Truly I tell you, just as you did it to one of the least of these who are members of my family, you did it to me." (Matthew 25:35–40)

Once they are separated, the people who helped others will be rewarded with eternal life! Jesus said:

But I say to you that listen, love your enemies, do good to those who hate you, bless those who curse you, pray for those who abuse you. If anyone strikes you on the cheek, offer the other also; and from anyone who takes away your coat do not withhold even your shirt. Give to everyone who begs from you; and if anyone takes away your goods, do not ask for them again. **Do to others as you would have them do to you.**

If you love those who love you, what credit is that to you? For even sinners love those who love them. If you do good to those who do good to you, what credit is that to you? For even sinners do the same. If you lend to those from whom you hope to receive, what credit is that to you? Even sinners lend to sinners, to receive as much again. But love your enemies, do good, and lend, expecting nothing in return. Your reward will be great, and you will be children of the Most High; for [H]e is kind to the ungrateful and the wicked.

Be merciful, just as your Father is merciful. Do not judge, and you will not be judged; do not condemn, and you will not be condemned. Forgive, and you will be forgiven; give, and it will be given to you. A good measure, pressed down, shaken together, running over, will be put into your lap; **for the measure you give will be the measure you get back.** *(Luke 6:27–38, emphasis added)*

Thus, the Christian Capitalist realizes that giving without any expectation of return is what Jesus expects of His followers. The reward for that conduct is not accolades or recognition here on Earth, but the eternal riches of Heaven!

The Wedding Banquet

The people of Israel, like modern individuals, really loved to celebrate a wedding. Weddings were some of the few occasions that people would put together big feasts and parties outside of religious holidays. Depending on the financial means of the parents of the bride and groom, these could be very expensive events, lasting multiple days.

Just like today, destination weddings were very popular. Jesus chose a wedding of some of His family friends at Cana to perform His first miracle and publicly announce His ministry. He also used a wedding as a setting to tell His apostles and followers about generosity and the importance of giving without expecting anything in return.

On one occasion when Jesus was going to the house of a leader of the Pharisees to eat a meal on the sabbath, they were watching [H]im closely. . . . When [H]e noticed how the guests chose the places of honor, [H]e told them a parable.

"When you are invited by someone to a wedding banquet, do not sit down at the place of honor, in case someone more distinguished than you has been invited by your host; and the host who invited both of you may come and say to you, 'Give this person your place,' and then in disgrace you would start to take the lowest place. But when you are invited, go and sit down at the lowest place, so that when your host comes, he may say to you, 'Friend, move up higher'; then you will be honored in the presence of all who sit at the table with you. For all who exalt themselves will be humbled, and those who humble themselves will be exalted."

*He said also to the one who had invited [H]im, "When you give a luncheon or a dinner, do not invite your friends or your brothers or your relatives or rich neighbors, in case they may invite you in return, and you would be repaid. **But when you give a banquet,*** *invite the poor, the crippled, the lame, and the blind. And you will be blessed, because they cannot repay you, for you will be repaid at the resurrection of the righteous." (Luke 14:1, 7–14, emphasis added)*

Give to Caesar What Is Caesar's

In addition to reminding His followers about generosity without expectation, Jesus also reminds everyone that giving must include civic responsibility. While He tells His apostles and followers to give generously to the poor, He also lets them know that the Earthly things are often best left to the Earth.

Then the Pharisees went out and laid plans to trap [H]im in [H]is words. They sent their disciples to [H]im along with the Herodians. "Teacher," they said, "we know that you are a man of integrity and that you teach the way of God in accordance with the truth. You aren't swayed by others, because you pay no attention to who they are. Tell us then, what is your opinion? Is it right to pay the imperial tax to Caesar or not?"

But Jesus, knowing their evil intent, said, "You hypocrites, why are you trying to trap me? Show me the coin used for paying the tax." They brought [H]im a denarius, and [H]e asked them, "Whose image is this? And whose inscription?" "Caesar's," they replied. Then [H]e said to them, "So give back to Caesar what is Caesar's, and to God what is God's." When they heard this, they were amazed. So they left [H]im and went away. (Matthew 22:15–22).

People should follow God's will by placing emphasis on the Kingdom of Heaven. By paying taxes and following the rule of law, everyone can still give to God.

In the story of His visit to the home of Mary and Martha, Jesus tells us that **we will always have the poor**, and it is all right to glorify Him with our wealth:

Six days before the Passover Jesus came to Bethany, the home of Lazarus, whom [H]e had raised from the dead. There they gave a dinner for [H]im. Martha served, and Lazarus was one of those at the table with [H]im. Mary took a pound of costly perfume, anointed Jesus's feet, and wiped them with her hair. The house was filled with the fragrance of the perfume.

But Judas Iscariot, one of [H]is disciples (the one who was about to betray [H]im), said, "Why was this perfume not sold for three hundred denarii and the money given to the poor?" (He said this not because he cared about the poor, but because he was a thief; he kept the common purse and used to steal what was put into it.) Jesus said, "Leave her alone. She bought it so that she might keep it for the day of my burial. You always have the poor with you, but you do not always have me." (John 12:1–8)

The Christian Capitalist understands that this story is important for two reasons. First, we will always have the poor, at any time and around the world. Second, we must be good stewards of the things that have been entrusted to us by God and share them with the poor to the best of our abilities. While we may not be able to help all the poor and needy around the world, we can do our best to help those we encounter at the gate.

Joseph of Arimathea—The First Christian Capitalist

The Gospels conclude with Christ serving in the role of servant leader, washing the disciples' feet, and taking on the cross.

This lesson had an immediate impact on Joseph of Arimathea, who took on the mantle of servant leader at a critical moment.

As they conclude the story of the passion of Jesus, including His torture and death, Matthew, Mark, Luke, and John all mention Joseph of Arimathea. At the end of the Friday that Roman leader Pontius Pilate ordered Jesus put to death (now referred to by Christians as "Good Friday"), Joseph went to visit Pilate and asked Pilate for Jesus's body. Pilate granted this request, and Joseph then went to Calvary (the hill where Jesus was crucified) and took Jesus down from the cross to prepare Him for burial.

The people of ancient Israel didn't have cemeteries like today. Instead, wealthier families had caves that they used for tombs. Jesus's family was not wealthy. Once Mary, mother of Jesus, and Mary Magdalene had prepared Jesus's body for burial, Joseph of Arimathea took Jesus and laid Him in Joseph's family tomb. From there, Jesus rose from the dead three days later on the day that Christians now refer to as Easter.

Thus, Joseph of Arimathea became a saint in the Church because, within hours of Jesus's death, he was the first person to provide his financial resources for the benefit of another in the name of Jesus Christ. Through his generous giving to the poor and needy, Joseph of Arimathea became the first Christian Capitalist, kicking off this movement long before either Christianity or capitalism even existed!

Time and time again throughout Holy Scripture, whether it's the Torah, the Psalms, or the prophets, we hear God's Word that we are to help the needy, give to the poor, heal the sick, and take care of those who are on the margins. The best way for Christian Capitalists to do that is by sharing wealth with others. We can't serve God and wealth, but we can use wealth to help others and follow God's will!

PART III

EARLY CHRISTIAN LIFE OF WORK AND GIVING

During His time on Earth, Jesus Christ taught people about the Kingdom of Heaven, including how to work and how to give. Even then, the apostles often had difficulty understanding what Jesus was trying to tell them, even after He explained the message to them carefully.

Things didn't get any easier once Jesus ascended into Heaven. Almost immediately after His death, resurrection, and glorious ascension, Christians began arguing over what Jesus meant with His various teachings, including those on work and giving. In this next part, we will discuss early Christian interpretations of His message, including communal living arrangements, as well as early lessons on work and giving. Two thousand years later, the Christian Capitalist has many ancient examples of work and giving to help guide the way in the modern world.

THE BEGINNING OF THE CHRISTIAN CAPITALIST ETHIC

Saul was a hardworking, driven man. He was a Pharisee, which means that he was an elite part of Jewish culture and a very strict follower of the law of Moses. He described himself as blameless in terms of his adherence to the strict statutes and ordinances of the time, and he also hated the followers of Christ. Because so much of Jesus's message focused on putting the relationship with God above adherence to the Mosaic law, Saul simply couldn't stand Christians. They flagrantly violated the law that he dedicated himself to following his entire life. On behalf of the high priest in the temple, he persecuted Christians throughout Jerusalem and Judea.

On the road to Damascus, while in the process of pursuing Christians to try and wipe out that early Christian community, Saul had a miraculous conversion experience. A bright light knocked him off his horse, and he heard the voice of Jesus ask him: "Saul, why do you hurt me?" Saul was immediately blinded, so his men took him to Damascus and laid him in a house. An angel visited a resident of Damascus named Ananias, and he tasked him with the mission of returning sight to Saul. When Ananias laid his hands on Saul's eyes, and his sight was restored, Saul's conversion was complete. He arose from the floor in that house in Damascus a new man, and a new follower of Christ with a new name—Paul.

Paul was as energetic and hardworking at spreading the Good News as he had been at stomping out early Christian communities! After some very touchy situations, in which he convinced early Christians that he was no longer against them, he began to gain the trust of Peter and the other apostles. More importantly, Paul traveled extensively to spread the Good News. Over four separate journeys throughout the Mediterranean region, Paul established churches and Christian communities, visited and wrote to those communities, and, as any modern pastor would, took care of those churches he had planted as if he had planted beautiful trees.

The letters that Paul wrote to those early Christian communities form the bulk of the New Testament after the Gospels and Acts of the Apostles. For the Christian Capitalist, they also provide ample support for the foundation of the Christian Capitalist Ethic. Paul worked hard and gave generously, and he encouraged other Christians to do the same!

Paul loved to work, and he encouraged others to work. Just as God created the universe and Jesus continued God's work of creation during His ministry, Peter, Paul, and the other apostles continued that work by growing the early Church and Christian communities around the Mediterranean region. As Paul planted churches and continued his travels, he would frequently pause to write a letter back to those communities. One of the themes of those letters was encouragement to continue the work that Jesus started by continuing to spread the Good News!

As Paul wrote letters of encouragement to early Church leaders, he continued to labor in the name of Christ and develop communities of Christians based on love. One of Paul's closest associates was Timothy, whom Paul frequently entrusted with important missions for the early Church. If Paul had a right-hand man beyond Luke, his physician and scribe, it may well have been Timothy. Paul eventually sent Timothy to a new church to help its development efforts, while he continued his travels and planting churches in other areas.

In his first letter to Timothy, Paul described the theme of this book and laid out the Christian Capitalist Ethic:

> *As for those who in the present age are rich, command them not to be haughty, or to set their hopes on the*

uncertainty of riches, but rather on God who richly pro-
vides us with everything for our enjoyment. They are to
do good, to be rich in good works, generous, and ready
to share, thus storing up for themselves the treasure of
a good foundation for the future, so that they may take
hold of the life that really is life. (1 Timothy 6:17–19)

To the Christian Capitalist, these words ring true today. It is critical for Christian Capitalists, especially those who have financial means, to share the blessings that God has given them with the world in the name of Jesus Christ. Just as Paul told Timothy two millennia ago, it's critical for the rich to carry on the work of Jesus by supporting those in need.

CHAPTER 7

COMMUNAL LIVING EXPERIMENTS

Early Christians experimented with a variety of ways to live together once Jesus ascended into Heaven. Several dynamics served as the catalyst for early Christians to form communities together: (1) common interest in building a community based on the principles Jesus taught them; (2) safety concerns due to the threat of persecution by the Jewish religious elite at the time, as well as the Romans; and (3) the desire to develop home bases for sending missionaries out into the world to proclaim the Good News. While there were many different ways to live as a Christian in the first century, Holy Scripture gives us a few examples.

THE NEW COMMUNITY OF CHRISTIANS LOVES AND GROWS IN *KOINONIA*

Koinonia is the ancient Greek word for a community of close-knit people. The first Christians that Luke describes in Acts of the Apostles consisted of individuals such as these, a tight-knit group who shared the Gospel and everything else they had. The result was a community that grew rapidly.

> *They devoted themselves to the apostles' teaching and fellowship, to the breaking of bread and the prayers. Awe came upon everyone, because many wonders and signs were being done by the apostles. All who believed were together and had all things in common; they would sell their possessions and goods and distribute the proceeds to all, as any had need. Day by day, as they spent much time together in the temple, they broke bread at home and ate their food with glad and generous hearts, praising God and having the goodwill of all the people. And day by day the Lord added to their number those who were being saved. (Acts 2:42–47)*

This early Christian community sounded almost utopian. Everybody was happy, everyone was working together to spread the Good News, and everyone was working toward the common goal of establishing the Church after Jesus's hard work to get things started. Peter and the other apostles took this work very seriously; they committed their lives to it. Ultimately, all of them lost their lives in their efforts to follow Jesus's Great Commission: go forth and make disciples of all nations. In this early Christian community, they focused on gaining new members of the Church and doing what they could to live like Jesus.

> *Now the whole group of those who believed were of one heart and soul, and no one claimed private ownership of any possessions, but everything they owned was held in common. With great power the apostles gave their testimony to the resurrection of the Lord Jesus, and great grace was upon them all. There was not a needy person*

among them, for as many owned lands or houses sold them and brought the proceeds of what was sold. They laid it at the apostles' feet, and it was distributed to each as any had need. (Acts 4:32–35)

Furthermore, this description of the early Christian community was likely a firsthand account. Luke wrote his Gospel and Acts of the Apostles as a two-volume set. As one of the first disciples who committed his entire life to the Church, although he was not part of the original twelve apostles, Luke had firsthand knowledge of the early Church and committed much of that record to writing in the Acts of the Apostles. In Acts, we learn about early Christian communities, the work of Peter to form the early Church with the other apostles, and stories of Paul's great journeys around the Mediterranean to spread the Good News.

TROUBLE WITH EARLY CHRISTIAN COMMUNAL LIVING

The description of the early Christian community in Acts tells us that everyone lived and worked for the common good. For the Christian Capitalist, it also describes an important characteristic of this early community that seems jarring now: everyone held everything in common and did not have any private property. For the Christian Capitalist, this provision in Holy Scripture is critical to know and understand.

Every Christian Capitalist knows that not all Christians are, indeed, capitalists. Millions of Christians around the world today, and certainly historically, are followers of Jesus but believe that a socialist economic and government system is the best method to achieve the life that Jesus wants us to live.

Early Christian communal living, used by some as a model for socialism in the future, shows three major flaws in the system. First, communal living didn't last long in Jerusalem because it wasn't sustainable. Second, we have no record from Holy Scripture that any other communities tried to live in common without private property ownership. In fact, Acts is full of references to Paul's visits to capitalist economies that were starting Christian churches. Third, communal living hasn't worked since then.

First, this utopian version of Christian society in Jerusalem, led by Peter and the other apostles, likely lasted no more than a few years after Pentecost. Pentecost was the miraculous event in which tongues of flame appeared above the heads of the apostles, and they all began speaking in different languages. This miracle allowed the apostles to go out into the world and spread the Good News, as Jesus instructed them.

The early experiment in communal living in Jerusalem was short-lived. The early Christian community had problems with the common distribution of food as it continued to grow. Luke describes a community that was not sustainable.

> Now during those days, when the disciples were increasing in number, the Hellenists complained against the Hebrews because their widows were being neglected in the daily distribution of food. And the twelve called together the whole community of the disciples and said, "It is not right that we should neglect the [W]ord of God in order to wait on tables. Therefore, friends, select from among yourselves seven men of good standing, full of the Spirit and of wisdom, whom we may appoint to this task, while we, for our part, will devote ourselves to prayer and to serving the word." What they said pleased the whole community, and they chose Stephen, a man full of faith and the Holy Spirit, together with Philip, Prochorus, Nicanor, Timon, Parmenas, and Nicolaus, a proselyte of Antioch. They had these men stand before

*the apostles, who prayed and laid their hands on them.
(Acts 6:1–6)*

The Hellenists in this story were Jews likely born outside of Israel, who primarily spoke Greek. They complained that Peter's distribution of food to the native Hebrew widows was disproportionate to the Hellenist widows, and this caused discontent in the whole community.

As Matthew Henry, the great Enlightenment biblical scholar, wrote in 1710 about this early Christian community: "A great deal of money was gathered for the relief of the poor, but, as often happens in such cases, it was impossible to please everybody in the laying of it out."[1] Rev. Henry's comment three hundred years ago about people two thousand years ago seems entirely relevant today. In attempting to provide mass assistance to the poor, it was impossible to make everyone happy, just as it is now. This is such a true statement that it is likely a human condition. Going back to ancient times, when God used Moses to lead the people of Israel out of slavery in Egypt, the first thing they did on the other side of the Red Sea was complain about being hungry!

As for those Christians who could provide for themselves, however, it appears from Holy Scripture that they went back to living as they had before this great experiment in communal living in Jerusalem began. As the earlier quotation from Luke notes, the apostles quickly addressed the problem administering food to the widows by naming seven deacons to serve the poor, and this solution "pleased the whole community."

The story of Ananias and Sapphira seems harsh to modern readers, but it surely sent a striking message to early Christians living in this communal way. It is yet another sign that the communal living experiment was in trouble. Their fate sent a message to early Christians just as surely as future Marxist and communist governments later told their subjects: give everything to the common good of the people, or else!

*But a man named Ananias, with the consent of his wife
Sapphira, sold a piece of property; with his wife's knowledge, he kept back some of the proceeds, and brought
only a part and laid it at the apostles' feet. "Ananias,"
Peter asked, "why has Satan filled your heart to lie to
the Holy Spirit and to keep back part of the proceeds of
the land? While it remained unsold, did it not remain
your own? And after it was sold, were not the proceeds
at your disposal? How is it that you have contrived this
deed in your heart? You did not lie to us but to God!"
Now when Ananias heard these words, he fell down
and died. And great fear seized all who heard of it. The
young men came and wrapped up his body, then carried
him out and buried him.*

*After an interval of about three hours his wife came
in, not knowing what had happened. Peter said to her,
"Tell me whether you and your husband sold the land
for such and such a price." And she said, "Yes, that was
the price." Then Peter said to her, "How is it that you
have agreed together to put the Spirit of the Lord to
the test? Look, the feet of those who have buried your
husband are at the door, and they will carry you out."
Immediately she fell down at his feet and died. When
the young men came in they found her dead, so they
carried her out and buried her beside her husband. And
great fear seized the whole church and all who heard of
these things. (Act 5:1–11)*

Later, Paul tells the people of Corinth that God loves a cheerful giver. Apparently, God likewise condemned those that
were not forthright in their giving to this early community
of believers. Either way, this story of Ananias and Sapphira
was likely used for centuries by often ill-intentioned clergy to
cajole donations from their congregations.

The second reason that modern people should not point to early Christian communal living as a model for socialist living today is that neither Acts of the Apostles, nor any of the other books of the New Testament, provide an indication that other communities operated like the one Peter and the apostles started in Jerusalem immediately following Jesus's ascension.

Time and again, Paul would visit cities and towns around the Mediterranean region and find a variety of communities ranging from thriving port cities like Tyre and Caesarea Philippi to poor towns that were struggling to survive. None of these towns or communities seemed to embrace the notion of communal property ownership and division of goods based on a central figure determining what everyone needed. The experiment in Jerusalem seemed to be limited to that community, and as we discussed earlier, it didn't last for long.

The third reason that early Christian communal living provides a flawed model for socialist systems is that socialism (without some version of free enterprise) has not worked outside of a Christian community either. This book is about working and giving, not a history of the various forms of governments and economies around the world for the last two millennia. It is fair to note, however, that the biggest economies that were built on the principles of Karl Marx since World War II, the USSR (Soviet Union) and the People's Republic of China (PRC), have now gravitated away from socialism and moved in the direction of capitalism.

While neither the USSR nor the PRC was purely socialist as Marx envisioned that system, neither has now developed a purely capitalist system as that economic model has developed over time. Both nations have discovered that people want to work, earn compensation for the work that they perform, and accumulate wealth. Likewise, Christians in those nations are still inclined to give to others in need, just as the early Christians did.

CHRISTIANS SERVE EACH OTHER ACROSS COMMUNITIES

Joseph of Cyprus Sells a Field and Provides the Proceeds for the Church

The Good News that Peter and the other apostles spread around Jerusalem had an impact on hundreds, then thousands of people living in Jerusalem. This included Jews who were not native to Jerusalem or Judea who lived around the Mediterranean region. Cyprus, an island in the Aegean Sea between Turkey and Greece, had one of the first churches and developed a strong early Christian community. It also led to one of the first stories about a Christian reaching out to others outside of his community to give generously and assist them.

> *There was a Levite, a native of Cyprus, Joseph, to whom the apostles gave the name Barnabas (which means "son of encouragement"). He sold a field that belonged to him, then brought the money, and laid it at the apostles' feet. (Acts 4:36–37)*

Although Acts doesn't tell us where this field was located, it certainly shows that Joseph of Cyprus was motivated to be generous to help with the early Christian cause. It's also noteworthy that Joseph was a Levite. That means he was Jewish and from the tribe of Levi, which comprised the priestly elite in ancient Jewish culture. Of the twelve tribes of Israel that descended from Abraham, Isaac, and Jacob, the Levites were tasked with caring for the temple and providing priests to serve in the synagogues around the nation. This tribe was significant.

Therefore, Joseph of Cyprus took this extraordinary step of selling a field and providing the funds to the apostles of Jesus Christ. It was an early sign that Jesus's work to overturn the temple culture in Jerusalem had a lasting effect.

For Christian Capitalists, it also sends a clear message that anyone, from anywhere, can be motivated to work and give in the name of Jesus Christ if given the opportunity!

Christians in Antioch Led an Early Hunger Relief Project for Jerusalem

Although Jerusalem served as the headquarters of the early Church, the Good News spread like wildfire, and the population of Christians grew dramatically in the first few decades after Pentecost. Peter and his closest disciples focused on spreading the Good News and converting Jews to Christianity. Meanwhile, the other apostles took the message out into the world and left Israel far behind.

In his famous conversion, Saul became Paul after a miracle on the road to Damascus. This ended his role as a Jewish persecutor of early Christians and transformed him into an articulate and energetic voice for the message of Jesus Christ. In four separate trips, he traveled all over the Mediterranean region, spreading the Good News.

As he and the other apostles traveled, they left behind groups of Christians who formed churches and spread the Good News to others in their communities. Paul reached back out to those early churches in the form of letters that comprise a significant portion of the New Testament. Meanwhile, Luke, the author of the Gospel that bears his name and Acts of the Apostles, described Paul's adventures from an eyewitness account. Luke was Paul's physician and was with Paul almost every step of the way as he traveled. Although all the stories of the early Church don't directly involve Paul, they certainly reflect his mark on early Christian churches.

> *So it was that for an entire year they met with the church and taught a great many people, and it was in Antioch that the disciples were first called "Christians."*

At that time prophets came down from Jerusalem to Antioch. One of them named Agabus stood up and predicted by the Spirit that there would be a severe famine over all the world; and this took place during the reign of Claudius. The disciples determined that according to their ability, each would send relief to the believers living in Judea; this they did, sending it to the elders by Barnabas and Saul [Paul]. (Acts 11:26–30)

People Commit to the Way of Jesus without Regard to the Cost

As the Church began to grow, many people began to cast aside their belief in multiple gods and pagan ways. Likewise, people all over the Mediterranean region believed in a multitude of gods and what Acts described as "magic." For many, the Good News helped them cast aside these old ways and embrace the way, the truth, and the light of Jesus Christ. This would happen despite the cost of giving up those old things.

Also many of those who became believers confessed and disclosed their practices. A number of those who practiced magic collected their books and burned them publicly; when the value of these books was calculated, it was found to come to fifty thousand silver coins. So the word of the Lord grew mightily and prevailed. (Acts 19:18–20)

For the Christian Capitalist, the implication of the story is clear. No matter what the cost, whether it's measured in goods or in currency, the Good News of Jesus takes priority.

GOD USES PETER TO HELP THOSE WHO HELP OTHERS

Jesus told Peter that he was the rock upon which Jesus would build His Church. After Pentecost, Peter focused his ministry on Jerusalem and Judea, and God used him to preach the Good News and provide early examples to Christians of how to help one another.

Peter's Gift of Walking to the Beggar

Time and time again, as I head out into the world and meet people who are in need, their first request is for money. This lesson from Acts, however, tells the Christian Capitalist that money may not always be the best way to assist them. In modern terms, Peter literally provides a hand-up as opposed to a handout in the story below.

> *One day Peter and John were going up to the temple at the time of prayer—at three in the afternoon. And a man lame from birth was being carried in. People would lay him daily at the gate of the temple called the Beautiful Gate so that he could ask for alms from those entering the temple. When he saw Peter and John about to go into the temple, he asked them for alms. Peter looked intently at him, as did John, and said, "Look at us." And he fixed his attention on them, expecting to receive something from them.*
>
> *But Peter said,* ***"I have no silver or gold, but what I have I give you; in the name of Jesus Christ of Nazareth, stand up and walk."*** *And he took him by the right hand and raised him up; and immediately his feet and ankles were made strong. Jumping up, he stood and began to walk, and he entered the temple with them, walking and leaping and praising God. All the people saw him walking and praising God, and they recognized him as the one who used to sit and ask for alms at the Beautiful Gate of the temple; and they were filled with wonder and amazement at what had happened to him. (Acts 3:1–10, emphasis added)*

As the Christian Capitalist considers the best way to assist someone in need, therefore, they should be open to God's guidance. Sometimes, a hand-up not only is the best way to assist someone but is also the assistance that a person will appreciate and be able to use to improve their condition in the long term.

As his work around Jerusalem increased, Peter began to grow the early Church in that community and continue the work of Jesus. It wasn't long before God gave Peter the ability to perform miracles, including the ability to raise the dead! It is important to note that God didn't choose Peter randomly. God likewise had a very specific reason behind giving Peter the power to raise Tabitha from the grave.

Peter Raises Tabitha from the Dead to Continue Her Works of Charity

We know little about Tabitha from Holy Scripture, other than she lived near Joppa and died at presumably a young age. We know that Tabitha was a member of the early Church and had friends who loved her enough that they sent for Peter to come try and raise her from the dead. This act of desperation and love tells us that Tabitha would be greatly missed.

> *Now in Joppa there was a disciple whose name was Tabitha, which in Greek is Dorcas.* **She was devoted to good works and acts of charity.** *At that time she became ill and died. When they had washed her, they laid her in a room upstairs. Since Lydda was near Joppa, the disciples, who heard that Peter was there, sent two men to him with the request, "Please come to us without delay." So Peter got up and went with them; and when he arrived, they took him to the room upstairs. All the widows stood beside him, weeping and showing tunics*

and other clothing that Dorcas had made while she was with them.

Peter put all of them outside, and then he knelt down and prayed. He turned to the body and said, "Tabitha, get up." Then she opened her eyes, and seeing Peter, she sat up. He gave her his hand and helped her up. Then calling the saints and widows, he showed her to be alive. This became known throughout Joppa, and many believed in the Lord. Meanwhile he stayed in Joppa for some time with a certain Simon, a tanner. (Acts 9:36–43, emphasis added)

Most importantly, we know that Tabitha lived her life generously helping others. Of all the people that Peter likely raised, it's noteworthy to the Christian Capitalist that Acts highlights Peter's efforts to bring Tabitha back to life. Why would God empower Peter to perform this miracle? One theory for the Christian Capitalist is clear: God wanted her to continue her good works of charity in the community, so He sent Peter to bring her back from the dead. For modern Christian Capitalists, this message is important for two reasons. First, through the story of Tabitha's resurrection, God tells us that He wants us to be charitable to others as long as we are alive. Second, it tells Christian Capitalists that God recognizes their charitable efforts here on Earth.

In addition to raising people from the dead, God gave Peter the ability to baptize believers. Peter may have baptized thousands of people in the early years of the Christian movement. This was the primary method that he used to grow the population of the Church so rapidly. In one instance, however, God led Peter to baptize an entire household based on the charitable work of its members.

God Calls Peter to Baptize Cornelius and His Family Based on Cornelius's Charity

Of all the apostles, Peter is the one typically portrayed as having the biggest problem with Roman subjugation. To say the least, he was not a willing subject of the Empire! Furthermore, as the early Church grew, one of the first areas of dispute between the apostles was whether Jesus's ministry, and as a result, their efforts to spread the Good News, should be geared only toward the people of Israel or addressed to all people (what the apostles commonly referred to at the time as Gentiles). Initially, Peter advocated for spreading the Good News only to the Jews in Israel; God had another plan for Peter, however.

First, God sent an angel to him to instruct him that he was to spread the Good News to both Jews and Gentiles around the region. Second, the angel specifically told Peter to go to Cornelius's house. Peter must have been shocked! Peter would probably have rather baptized anyone other than a Roman. In particular, he certainly would have objected to baptizing a senior Roman officer. Cornelius was a centurion, which means that he led one hundred men in the occupation of Judea.

> In Caesarea there was a man named Cornelius, a centurion of the Italian Cohort, as it was called. He was a devout man who feared God with all his household; **he gave alms generously to the people and prayed constantly to God**. One afternoon at about three o'clock he had a vision in which he clearly saw an angel of God coming in and saying to him, "Cornelius." He stared at him in terror and said, "What is it, Lord?"
>
> He answered, "Your prayers and your alms have ascended as a memorial before God. Now send men to Joppa for a certain Simon who is called Peter; he is lodging with Simon, a tanner, whose house is by the seaside."

When the angel who spoke to him had left, he called two of his slaves and a devout soldier from the ranks of those who served him, and after telling them everything, he sent them to Joppa. (Acts 10: 1–8, emphasis added)

Acts tells us that Cornelius is not the typical Roman centurion. Instead, he is generous and kind, and he is charitable to Romans, Jews, and Gentiles alike. Once Cornelius's men went to Joppa and got Peter, he returned with them to Cornelius's home and baptized the household.

As a result, God's choice for Peter's first baptism of a Gentile is a clear one. Cornelius is not just a typical Roman officer: he is generous, kind and prayerful. By choosing Cornelius, God is teaching Peter that all people can be followers of Him on the path that Jesus established, even if they are Roman and pagan. Furthermore, God once again shows that He notices our work here on Earth. For the Christian Capitalist, the implication of this story is clear. God goes to great lengths not only to teach Peter that all people can be saved but that the charitable works done here on Earth are observed by God. God loves it when we take care of each other!

CHAPTER 8

EARLY CHRISTIAN TEACHING ON WORK

As we note at the beginning of this part, Paul summarizes the theme of this book in his first letter to Timothy. At the same time, he also develops the basis for the Christian Capitalist Ethic. The first component of this Ethic is hard work. Paul works hard and encourages others to do the same. In a speech to early Christians, for example, he reminds them that he is hardworking and self-sufficient: "You know for yourselves that I worked with my own hands to support myself and my companions" (Acts 20:34). Through his speeches and letters, as well as the work and writings of the other leaders of the early Church, Paul develops a theology of hard work.

PAUL SETS AN EXAMPLE FOR HARD WORK

Paul further continues to encourage early Christians to work hard. This work was indeed a labor of love as early Christians battled the forces that resisted the Good News. First, pagan cultures around the Mediterranean region were well set for hundreds, maybe even thousands, of years. As the merchants in Caesarea Philippi noted, there was money to be made in selling idols of worship, and this is just an example of the kind of entrenched paganism that Christianity battled in those early years. The second, stronger force from a political and military perspective, was the Roman Empire. Not long after Pentecost and the development of these early churches, the people of Israel had had enough of Roman rule and rebelled against it. The Romans quickly squashed the rebellion in 72 AD, burning the temple that had been rebuilt 600 years earlier by Nehemiah and unofficially ending the temple culture that Jesus had worked to reform and overthrow by spiritual means.

These twin forces of paganism and Roman might have created significant obstacles for the early Church, but they were ultimately overcome by hard work and the labor of love.

> *Let it be known to you therefore, my brothers, that through this man forgiveness of sins is proclaimed to you; by this Jesus everyone who believes is set free from all those sins from which you could not be freed by the law of Moses. Beware, therefore, that what the prophets said does not happen to you: "Look, you scoffers! Be amazed and perish, for in your days I am doing a work, a work that you will never believe, even if someone tells you." (Acts 13:38–41)*

Paul harkened back to the ancient prophets who had people scoff at and reject them, yet they persisted. In addition to working hard on behalf of the Lord, by spreading the Good News and planting churches around the Mediterranean region, Paul also worked to support himself.

After this, Paul left Athens and went to Corinth. There he found a Jew named Aquila, a native of Pontus, who had recently come from Italy with his wife Priscilla, because Claudius had ordered all Jews to leave Rome. Paul went to see them, and, because he was of the same trade, he stayed with them, and they worked together— by trade they were tentmakers. (Acts 18:1–3)

Setting an example for itinerant pastors for the next two thousand years, Paul traveled around the region and, where he could, stopped to work and make money to buy food and necessities for himself and his travel companions, whom he called "co-workers for the Kingdom of God" (see Colossians 4:11). Paul encouraged other early Christians to follow that example. He essentially put them in the footsteps of continuing the work of Jesus, focusing on the abundance of God's love. "Therefore, my beloved, be steadfast, immovable, **always excelling in the work of the Lord,** because you know that in the Lord your labor is not in vain" (1 Corinthians 15:58, emphasis added).

It's difficult to overstate the emphasis that Paul put on hard work, and how he tried to lead early Christians by his own example. In his letter to the Colossians, he described his work to spread the Good News around the ancient world: "For this I toil and struggle with all the energy that [H]e powerfully inspires within me" (Colossians 1:29).

The Christian Capitalist likewise feels the energy that God powerfully inspires, so they can toil and struggle to do the work that God calls each person to do. That calling differs with each person based on the gifts that God has provided.

LESSONS ON WORK

At the same time Paul was working hard to set an example for early Christians about how to work hard, he was also writing letters to other Christian communities, encouraging them to do the same.

He encouraged early Christians to work hard to grow the Kingdom of Heaven and consider that work a labor of love. Specifically, he encouraged them to grow the Church in a particular town or community and to grow it around the world. With this encouragement, Paul provided a lesson to the early Christians on work that still resounds today: "We always give thanks to God for all of you and mention you in our prayers, constantly remembering before our God and Father your work of faith and labor of love and steadfastness of hope in our Lord Jesus Christ" (1 Thessalonians 1:2–3).

Paul encouraged Christians to work hard and support themselves because that's what God wants them to do. Hard work, as we discussed previously, was first shown to man in the creation story, and this hard work by Christians at the time was the way that Paul felt could glorify God and move a person closer to righteousness. That hard work started with loving each other:

> *Now concerning love of the brothers and sisters, you do not need to have anyone write to you, for you yourselves have been taught by God to love one another. . . . But we urge you, beloved, to do so more and more, to aspire to live quietly, to mind your own affairs, and to work with your hands, as we directed you, so that you may behave properly toward outsiders and be dependent on no one. (1 Thessalonians 4:9–12)*

Once again, Paul led by example in this regard: "You remember our labor and toil, brothers and sisters; we worked night and day, so that we might not burden any of you while we proclaimed to you the [G]ospel of God" (1 Thessalonians 2:9). Paul likewise encouraged early Christians to work hard and follow the example of the leaders of the early Church, who worked hard as well. As leaders in any time and any area of life will say: lead by example. Paul knew this, too, and he expected early Christians to respect their leaders because of their hard work.

> *But we appeal to you, brothers and sisters, to respect those who labor among you, and have charge of you in the Lord and admonish you;* **esteem them very highly in love because of their work.** *Be at peace among yourselves. And we urge you, beloved, to admonish the idlers, encourage the fainthearted, help the weak, be patient with all of them. (1 Thessalonians 5:12–14, emphasis added)*

Today, Paul would likely be described as a workaholic. As is so often the case with workaholics, they tend to emphasize the value of work and encourage others to work hard. The flip side of the coin is also true. They also criticize those who they perceive as not working hard. Paul takes this criticism one step further and instructs early Christians to ostracize those "idle" members of the community and tell them that, if someone won't work, they shouldn't eat!

> *Now we command you, beloved, in the name of our Lord Jesus Christ, to keep away from believers who are living in idleness and not according to the tradition that they received from us. For you yourselves know how you ought to imitate us; we were not idle when we were with you, and we did not eat anyone's bread without pay-ing for it; but* **with toil and labor we worked night and day, so that we might not burden any of you.** *This was not because we do not have that right, but in order to give you an example to imitate. For even when we were with you, we gave you this command: Anyone*

*unwilling to work should not eat. For we hear that
some of you are living in idleness, mere busybodies, not
doing any work. Now such persons we command and
exhort in the Lord Jesus Christ to do their work quietly
and to earn their own living. (2 Thessalonians 3:6–12,
emphasis added)*

Notwithstanding the harshness of this lesson by today's standards, Paul's instructions on work to the people of Thessalonica still resound. The Christian Capitalist understands that
hard work, no matter what role the worker plays in a business
or other venture, is the key to following the path of Christ.

GOOD WORKS

Paul was the primary voice for early Christians about work,
but he wasn't the only one. Joseph and Mary had several other
children besides Jesus, according to Holy Scripture. The most
prominent was James, a Jewish teacher or *rabbi*, who was slow
to embrace Jesus's teachings.

After the resurrection and ascension, however, James became more involved with Peter and the other apostles, eventually gaining a leadership role in the early Church. In Acts of
the Apostles, Luke tells us that James was involved in one of
the first significant meetings of early Christians. This council
helped resolve some of the early debates about how to carry
forth the Good News out into the world.

Most biblical scholars believe that James was the author
of the book in the New Testament that carries his name, and
he has a lot to offer the Christian Capitalist to consider. While
Paul set a great example for hard work and implored early
Christians to do likewise, he also developed a theology based
on hard work using the gifts that God gives every person.
Most of the time, Paul's instructions about work focused on

mirroring the kind of work that he did, namely, growing the early Church.

James's focus, however, is broader. Instead of concentrating specifically on growing the Church and building early communities, James encouraged early Christians in his letter to be "doers of the word." By that, he meant that early Christians should spread the Good News in all that they did:

> *But be **doers of the word**, and not merely hearers who deceive themselves. For if any are hearers of the word and not doers, they are like those who look at themselves in a mirror; for they look at themselves and, on going away, immediately forget what they were like. (James 1:22–24, emphasis added).*

This notion of being "doers of the word" is summarized by Paul in his first letter to the Thessalonians: "See that none of you repays evil for evil, but always seek to do good to one another and to all" (1 Thessalonians 5:15). Doing good for others is the essence of the Second Commandment from Jesus: love one another as He loved us.

This was also a way to put the Word of God into action. The early Christians were tasked with building new churches in communities all around the Mediterranean region. Fundamentally, however, they focused their efforts on spreading the Good News of the Kingdom of God. Thus, the good word and good work were indivisible: "Now may our Lord Jesus Christ himself and God our Father, who loved us and through grace gave us eternal comfort and good hope, comfort your hearts and **strengthen them in every good word and work**" (2 Thessalonians 2:16-17, emphasis added).

In his letter to the people of Ephesus, Paul takes this one step further and states that we are created in Christ Jesus for good works. Paul summarizes the theme of the first chapter of this book, that Christian Capitalists believe that we are created in God's image to work, by stating: "For we are what [H]e has made us, **created in Christ Jesus for good works**, which God prepared beforehand to be our way of life" (Ephesians 2:10, emphasis added).

Paul tells the people of Corinth the meaning of good works in his first letter to them, "So, whether you eat or drink, or whatever you do, do everything for the glory of God. Give no offense to Jews or to Greeks or to the church of God, just as I try to please everyone in everything I do, not seeking my own advantage, but that of many, so that they may be saved" (1 Corinthians 10:31–33). Seeking the advantage of others is a succinct way to summarize that Second Commandment of Jesus: love your neighbor as yourself.

The result of these good works would not only lead to the benefit of others and the worker (as described more fully later) but also to a deeper understanding of God and, ultimately, wisdom. "For this reason, since the day we heard it, we have not ceased praying for you and asking that you may be filled with the knowledge of God's will in all spiritual wisdom and understanding, so that you may **lead lives worthy of the Lord, fully pleasing to [H]im, as you bear fruit in every good work and as you grow in the knowledge of God**" (Colossians 1:9–10, emphasis added).

Finally, James connects work and faith. Without one, he maintains that you can't have the other.

> *What good is it, my brothers and sisters, if you say you have faith but do not have works? Can faith save you? If a brother or sister is naked and lacks daily food, and one of you says to them, "Go in peace; keep warm and eat your fill," and yet you do not supply their bodily needs, what is the good of that? So faith by itself, if it has no*

*works, is dead. But someone will say, "You have faith and I have works." Show me your faith apart from your works, and **I by my works will show you my faith.** (James 2:14–18, emphasis added)*

Christian Capitalists, therefore, work hard for others because of their faith and, by that work, show everyone their faith.

GOD CALLS EACH PERSON TO USE THE GIFTS HE HAS GIVEN

Christian Capitalists likewise feel the energy that God powerfully inspires, so they can toil and struggle to do the work that God calls each person to do. That calling differs with each person based on the gifts that God has provided. Through prayer and reflection, Christian Capitalists can grow closer to God by using the gifts that He has provided to perform good works: "However that may be, let each of you lead the life that the Lord has assigned, to which God called you. This is my rule in all the churches" (1 Corinthians 7:17).

In his second letter to Timothy, Paul creates an important analogy for early Christians considering how to use their gifts to perform good works and lead the life God calls them. In God's kitchen, His people are special utensils: "In a large house there are utensils not only of gold and silver but also of wood and clay, some for special use, some for ordinary. All who cleanse themselves of the things I have mentioned will become special utensils, dedicated and useful to the owner of the house, **ready for every good work**" (2 Timothy 2:20–21, emphasis added).

Early Christians were building churches in their communities, and collectively, the Church was growing rapidly around the ancient world. In his letter to the Christians in the Church in Rome, Paul introduces an important theological concept based on the teachings of Jesus: every believer is part of the body of Christ, which is the Church. More importantly, for the purposes of the Christian Capitalist, each member of the body of Christ has unique gifts that make that body complete: "We have gifts that differ according to the grace given to us: prophecy, in proportion to faith; ministry, in ministering; the teacher, in teaching; the exhorter, in exhortation; the giver, in generosity; the leader, in diligence; the compassionate, in cheerfulness" (Romans 12:6–8).

Of course, Christian Capitalists likewise understand that when Paul talks about the giver having the gift of generosity, that applies to the efforts that they take today to share the blessings that God has provided them with the poor and needy. In his first letter to the people of Corinth, Paul further describes the Kingdom of God as a building, and each Christian has an important role to play once Jesus Christ lays the foundation. Ultimately, all the work that Christians do is both the result of God's blessing and attributes to the Kingdom of Heaven.

> *So neither the one who plants nor the one who waters is anything, but only God who gives growth. The one who plants and the one who waters have a common purpose, and each will receive wages according to the labor of each. For we are God's servants, working together; you are God's field, God's building. (1 Corinthians 3:7–9)*

GOD AT WORK IN US WHEN WE WORK

Every believer has different gifts from God, and every believer uses those gifts as part of the body of Christ, which is the Church. Beyond simply recognizing that those gifts come from God, Paul later explains to the people of Corinth that God is at work in everyone. In addition to providing these gifts and talents to each person, God activates those gifts through the Holy Spirit. The gifts vary widely, but ultimately each gift becomes the vehicle through which each person serves God and the world.

> *Now there are varieties of gifts, but the same Spirit; and there are varieties of services, but the same Lord; and there are varieties of activities, but it is the same God who activates all of them in everyone.* **To each is given the manifestation of the Spirit for the common good.**
>
> *To one is given through the Spirit the utterance of wisdom, and to another the utterance of knowledge according to the same Spirit, to another faith by the same Spirit, to another gifts of healing by the one Spirit, to another the working of miracles, to another prophecy, to another the discernment of spirits, to another various kinds of tongues, to another the interpretation of tongues. All these are activated by one and the same Spirit, who allots to each one individually just as the Spirit chooses. (1 Corinthians 12:8–11, emphasis added; see also 1 Corinthians 12:31)*

The Christian Capitalist recognizes that this list of gifts is a skill set to be used in business. Each one of these spiritual gifts can enhance or extend the abilities that the Christian Capitalist brings to the business and thus brings the Holy Spirit into a workplace or business venture to serve the will of God. Only through prayer and reflection can Christian Capitalists determine what this means for each particular circumstance. Being open to the Holy Spirit in one's life is the key to this first step, **"for it is God who is at work in you, enabling you both to will and to work for [H]is good pleasure"** (Philippians 2:13, emphasis added).

Every Christian has the duty to spread the Gospel, and the work that Christians accomplish in the world is the way that that Gospel gets spread. "We also constantly give thanks to God for this, that when you received the [W]ord of God that you heard from us, you accepted it not as a human word but as what it really is, God's [W]ord, which is also at work in you believers" (1 Thessalonians 2:13). Using the gifts provided by the Holy Spirit and energized by God, Christians have changed the world with this powerful combination, and Christian Capitalists recognize that they can continue to do so by recognizing that God has equipped them in this way.

Life can be hard, and even believers who trust in God and enjoy the riches of the blessings that God has provided them can fall on tough times. In his journeys around the Mediterranean, Paul found that spreading the Good News often left him at odds with the people in a particular community, that the store of food and resources he had compiled ran dry, or that he simply exhausted himself and his mission. Either way, he became content with what he had and did not let that interfere with him accomplishing the mission that God gave him.

> *Not that I am referring to being in need; for I have learned to be content with whatever I have. I know what it is to have little, and I know what it is to have plenty. In any and all circumstances I have learned the secret of being well-fed and of going hungry, of having plenty and of being in need.* ***I can do all things through [H]im who strengthens me.*** *(Philippians 4:11–13, emphasis added)*

No task is too tall for the Christian Capitalist because with the power of the one true God, and the talents activated by the Holy Spirit, every Christian Capitalist can embrace Paul's statement of faith.

This notion that God is at work in all Christians leads to one of the fundamental tenets of the Christian Capitalist, which is that doing the work of God leads to riches of wisdom, regardless of whether it brings material wealth. "To them God chose to make known how great among the Gentiles are the riches of the glory of this mystery, which is Christ in you, the hope of glory. It is He whom we proclaim, warning every-one and teaching everyone in all wisdom, so that we may pres-ent everyone mature in Christ" (Colossians 1:27–28).

Business ventures risk time, resources, and capital. Not-withstanding the wisdom that comes with a closer relation-ship with God as Paul described to the people of Colossae, Christian Capitalists understand that the nature of business is insecure and that a new business venture always poses risks. This is why Christian Capitalists, regardless of their position in that venture, continue to lean on God to help them adapt and overcome the challenges of industry.

> *Come now, you who say, "Today or tomorrow we will go to such and such a town and spend a year there, doing business and making money." Yet you do not even know what tomorrow will bring. What is your life? For you are a mist that appears for a little while and then van-ishes. Instead you ought to say, "If the Lord wishes, we will live and do this or that." (James 4:13–15)*

James then proposes every move the Christian Capitalist makes should be guided by God. Many Christians, even today, pray continuously to God for guidance on even the smallest mat-ters in life. They do this especially when something big comes along, like taking on a new job, moving to a new community, or the like; people pray to God for guidance so that they can determine His will for them in their lives.

The Christian Capitalist recognizes that James raises a great point about the power of prayer in all business ventures. Even when data may not support a particular decision or projections based on historical experience might otherwise dictate, Christian Capitalists must pray to God for guidance in these business ventures to ensure that they have set the business venture on the right path. A good businessperson can't ignore good information. Prayer and reflection help put that information to good work.

BENEFITS OF WORK

In the previous parts of this book, the theology of work always includes some discussion of benefits to the worker. The New Testament lessons from Paul, James, and the other authors are no different. As they encourage early Christians to work hard to follow the path of Christ, build the Kingdom of Heaven, and serve others in their community, they conclude the discussion of work by describing the benefits that it brings to the worker. The most important benefit, of course, is a closer relationship with God through eternal life! "For [H]e will repay according to each one's deeds: to those who by patiently doing good seek for glory and honor and immortality, [H]e will give eternal life" (Romans 2:6–7).

God notices the good work that His people perform. Throughout Holy Scripture, authors have told us that good work will be noticed by God and rewarded. Early Christianity was no different. "So also good works are conspicuous; and even when they are not, they cannot remain hidden" (1 Timothy 5:25). As James instructed early Christians to be doers of the Word, he likewise promised them the benefits of their actions. "But those who look into the perfect law, the law of liberty, and persevere, being not hearers who forget but doers who act—**they will be blessed in their doing**" (James 1:25). God notices those who act on behalf of His word, namely, the Good News through His son Jesus Christ.

This Good News is a gift from God; it can be given but cannot be purchased. As Peter and John spread the Good News around Judea, they visit a community and begin baptizing people in the name of the Holy Spirit. A local trickster named Simon the Magician sees them and offers them silver coins in exchange for granting him the ability to perform the same miracles. As we might expect, that doesn't sit well with Peter!

> *"Give me also this power so that anyone on whom I lay my hands may receive the Holy Spirit." But Peter said to him [Simon the Magician], "May your silver perish with you, because you thought you could obtain God's gift with money! You have no part or share in this, for your heart is not right before God. Repent therefore of this wickedness of yours, and pray to the Lord that, if possible, the intent of your heart may be forgiven you. For I see that you are in the gall of bitterness and the chains of wickedness." (Acts 8:19–23)*

The promise of eternal life is heard in the name of Jesus to spread the Good News through their work, as the letter to the Hebrews describes:

> *For God is not unjust; [H]e will not overlook your work and the love that you showed for [H]is sake in serving the saints, as you still do. And we want each one of you to show the same diligence so as to realize the full assurance of hope to the very end, so that you may not become*

sluggish, but imitators of those who through faith and patience inherit the promises. (Hebrews 6:10–12)

As Paul wrote to the people of Philippi thanking them for the gifts that they had sent him, he connected the dots for them on the benefits of hard work and giving. Although many of the early churches sent Paul gifts, he specifically thanked the Philippians for their diligence in assisting him in their ministry and assured them that God would take note of their efforts.

The Christian Capitalist notes that Paul appreciated their gifts but did not do so in a self-centered way. As any good accountant or project manager would, he kept track of how all the early churches supported themselves and each other, including his ministry. Gifts to him were not so much to him as an individual, but those gifts created credits in their Heavenly account! Each gift to Paul, according to him, accrued to their heavenly benefit. Christian Capitalists understand that this heavenly accounting system works even today. Individuals who receive gifts from Christian Capitalists will most likely be appreciative. It is the act of giving, not the appreciation, that counts with God, however.

*You Philippians indeed know that in the early days of the [G]ospel, when I left Macedonia, no church shared with me in the matter of giving and receiving, except you alone. For even when I was in Thessalonica, you sent me help for my needs more than once. **Not that I seek the gift, but I seek the profit that accumulates to your account.** I have been paid in full and have more than enough; I am fully satisfied, now that I have received from Epaphroditus the gifts you sent, a fragrant offering, a sacrifice acceptable and pleasing to God. And my God will fully satisfy every need of*

yours according to [H]is riches in glory in Christ Jesus.
(Philippians 4:15–19, emphasis added)

As an aside, this notion should also help Christian Capitalists make sense of how to deal with situations in which they give a gift to a person in need who then is not appreciative. One of the hallmarks of Christian Capitalists is to give thanks to God by sharing the blessings that He has given them with the poor and needy, but not everyone appreciates the gifts that a Christian Capitalist gives. That Heavenly account, therefore, is one way to keep Christian Capitalists grounded when they love a neighbor but they are not loved in return.

CHAPTER 9

EARLY CHRISTIAN TEACHING ON GIVING

The early Christians worked hard to build churches around the Mediterranean region and build up supportive communities of common believers. Hard work was the engine for the formation and growth of these communities; giving and a sense of love through common purpose made them sustainable. While one of the first early Christian communities discussed in Acts is the onetime communal living experiment led by Peter, the majority of early Christian communities simply added the new element of followers of Jesus into preexisting economic and social systems.

While new churches were formed and leadership developed in and around those Christian communities, early Christians struggled to survive. Due to the power structures in place, including the Roman Empire, the Jewish temple hierarchy, and Gentile or pagan societies, the early Christians were left on the margins. Giving to one another in order to support the growth of the Church, as well as individual needs, was a key factor for Christians in the development of the early Church. As in previous generations of God's people, the theology of giving in the early Christian communities was based on the acknowledgment that all things are a gift from God.

The Torah, the prophets, the Psalms, and the Gospels laid the theological foundation for giving, and early Christians built on this. They recognized that all that is in the world is a gift from God who ". . . gives to all generously and ungrudgingly . . ." (James 1:5). God is the source of all gifts, and the Christian inclination to give to others is itself a gift from God. "Every generous act of giving, with every perfect gift, is from above, coming down from the Father of lights, with whom there is no variation or shadow due to change" (James 1:17).

God's greatest gift to humankind is His son Jesus. Paul tells the Romans in very specific financial terms: "For the wages of sin is death, but the free gift of God is eternal life in Christ Jesus our Lord" (Romans 6:23). Although people have to work to live, all they have to do to receive eternal life is accept that greatest of gifts, Jesus Christ.

LESSONS ON GIVING

Paul summarizes the theology of giving succinctly, and he puts the message straight back to the Good News spread by Jesus: "Bear one another's burdens, and in this way you will fulfill the law of Christ" (Galatians 6:2). In order to follow the path that Jesus sets out for everyone, the people have to share the blessings that God gives them and, as a result, share the burdens of others.

Above all, maintain constant love for one another, for love covers a multitude of sins. Be hospitable to one

> *another without complaining. Like good stewards of the manifold grace of God, serve one another with whatever gift each of you has received. (1 Peter 4:8–10)*

As Jesus sacrificed His own interest and well-being for everyone, Paul likewise encourages early Christians to do the same. Again, he puts this kind of mentality squarely on the path of following Jesus.

> *Do nothing from selfish ambition or conceit, but in humility regard others as better than yourselves.* **Let each of you look not to your own interest, but to the interests of others.** *Let the same mind be in you that was in Christ Jesus . . . (Philippians 2:3–5, emphasis added)*

Paul's instruction to regard others as better than ourselves is simply a way of saying what Jesus told us was the great Second Commandment: love your neighbor as yourself. If the core value of love is sacrifice, then it follows that sacrifice for a neighbor is the one true way to express that love. As Paul tells the Christians in Thessalonica in his first letter: ". . . always seek to do good to one another and to all" (1 Thessalonians 5:15). He also tells the people of Corinth: **"Do not seek your own advantage, but that of the other"** (1 Corinthians 10:24, emphasis added). Paul advocates that early Christians work hard to benefit the whole community, ". . . so that those who have come to believe in God may be careful to **devote themselves to good works; these things are excellent and profitable to everyone**" (Titus 3:8, emphasis added).

When working to benefit the community, Paul tells early Christians that their obligations start with other believers but end with everyone, even those unknown: ". . . love one another with mutual affection; outdo one another in showing honor . . . Contribute to the needs of the saints; extend hospitality to strangers" (Romans 12:10, 13). Peter likewise encourages early Christians to ". . . love one another deeply from the heart" (1 Peter 1:22).

Paul even reaches out to those who were outcast from Jewish society who chose to follow the path of Christ: "Thieves must give up stealing; rather let them labor and work honestly with their own hands, so as to have something to share with the needy" (Ephesians 4:28). Furthermore, Paul applies this lesson to those who are still learning to love their neighbor: "No, 'if your enemies are hungry, feed them; if they are thirsty, give them something to drink; for by doing this you will heap burning coals on their heads.' Do not be overcome by evil, but **overcome evil with good**" (Romans 12:20–21, emphasis added).

In his second letter to the early church in Corinth, Paul encourages the people to give to each other and support each other in the growth of that community. If there is a second theme of this book and core principle for the Christian Capitalist, he encapsulates it in the following passage:

> *Each of you must give as you have made up your mind, not reluctantly or under compulsion, for God loves a cheerful giver.* ***And God is able to provide you with every blessing in abundance, so that by always having enough of everything, you may share abundantly in every good work.*** *As it is written, "[H]e scatters abroad, [H]e gives to the poor; [H]is righteousness endures forever." (2 Corinthians 9:7–9, emphasis added; see also Psalm 112)*

Many Christians may have heard the first verse of this passage (about the cheerful giver) during a worship service at the time of the offertory. Pastors and priests of all denominations have quoted Paul and his message to the people of Corinth as a way to encourage the congregation to give as the offering plate passes by the members. Even in the electronic world of giving, churches frequently post this passage on their giving page to encourage people to input their credit cards or bank account information. For the Christian Capitalist, however, this notion of being a cheerful giver is only half the story. **The reason for the gift is the critical part of Paul's message, not the attitude of the giver.**

The Christian Capitalist notes that the verse following Paul's mention of the cheerful giver is the one that holds the most importance. By generously sharing the benefits that God has given us with those in need, the Christian Capitalist can follow the guidance that Paul set out for the people of Corinth 2,000 years ago!

Paul further elaborates on this point in a speech that he gave to the early Christians. "In all this I have given you an example that by such work we must support the weak, remembering the words of the Lord Jesus, for [H]e [H]imself said, 'It **is more blessed to give than to receive'**" (Acts 20:35, emphasis added). Today, many people quote Paul without knowing it when they talk about giving, especially around Christmas. Parents regularly cajole their children into focusing more on giving gifts than receiving them, especially when it comes to presents for siblings!

Paul's message about giving also indicates an early commitment by Christians to support others outside of their communities. In the previous chapter on work, Paul discussed a disaster relief effort organized by early Christians to send to Jerusalem. Based on other letters that he wrote to churches, there appears to likewise have been an organized system of giving in place that he referred to as "the collection for the saints."

In his first letter to the people of Corinth, he instructed them to follow the directions that he gave to the people in

Galatia: "On the first day of every week, each of you is to put aside and **save whatever extra you earn**, so that collections need not be taken when I come. And when I arrive, I will send any whom you approve with letters to take your gift to Jerusalem" (1 Corinthians 16:2–3, emphasis added).

Likewise, in his second letter to the people of Corinth, he discussed the generous giving from the people in the Church in Macedonia:

> *We want you to know, brothers and sisters, about the grace of God that has been granted to the churches of Macedonia; for during a severe ordeal of affliction, their abundant joy and their extreme poverty have overflowed in a wealth of generosity on their part. For, as I can testify, they voluntarily gave according to their means, and even beyond their means, begging us earnestly for the **privilege of sharing in this ministry to the saints** . . . (2 Corinthians 8:1–5, emphasis added)*

While encouraging eagerness to give, Paul recognized that some of these messages he sent to early Christians, in which he compared the generosity of churches, could be taken as creating a competitive spirit between the churches and their giving. He does try to downplay that kind of competition by recalling the Torah and the days when God brought manna from heaven to the people of Israel.

> *For if the eagerness is there, the gift is acceptable according to what one has—not according to what one does not have. I do not mean that there should be relief for others and pressure on you, but it is a question of a fair balance between your present abundance and their need, so that their abundance may be for your need, in order that there may be a fair balance. As it is written,*

"The one who had much did not have too much, and the one who had little did not have too little." (2 Corinthians 8:12-15)

As Moses and the people of Israel wandered the desert, God fed them manna from Heaven. Everyone had what they needed, and Paul harkened back to those days in encouraging early Christians to give to each other.

THE CHALLENGE OF BEING A CHEERFUL GIVER

Recently, I went to lunch with a friend in a part of town that I hadn't visited in quite some time. While the whole experience was familiar, it was still new and different because my GPS took a different route than usual. As I drove toward our lunch destination, I was struck by the number of people standing at the various intersections along my route begging for money. At several points along the way, each one of the four corners of an intersection had a man or a woman holding a handwritten sign asking for money.

My first encounter was with a man walking between the cars backed up on my side of a four-lane highway. Although it is certainly dangerous to walk between two rows of cars, stopped at a traffic light, he gave no indication he was concerned. Instead, he walked between the cars rotating between those on either side to make eye contact with the driver and ask for money. I rolled down my window and gave him a dollar bill. It didn't occur to me that I only had two bills left in my wallet after that, and I certainly didn't notice the amount of each.

After lunch, I was on my return trip home and taking the same route. This time, I pulled up at an intersection that was much busier and more congested but, likewise, was a four-lane highway with multiple cars in each direction leading to the traffic light. As in the previous instance, a man walked confidently between the rows of cars, asking for money from each driver. As I rolled down the front passenger window, I noticed this time that I was preparing to give him a ten-dollar bill. I thought to myself, "He certainly needs this more than me," and handed it to him.

Just a few minutes later, I had my final encounter that day before getting back to the interstate. I found myself on the opposite side of the same intersection where I had originally given the single dollar bill to the first man. This time, however, a woman walked down the road between the cars backed up at the traffic light. It was difficult to tell at first that she was a woman, because she was wearing a heavy coat and blue jeans. More importantly, she was tall and reed-thin. I knew, however, that her gaunt frame was not the result of heavy exercise or a running regimen. She was at least malnourished and probably starving. Nevertheless, as I rolled down the passenger window and opened my wallet, I paused.

The third and final bill in my wallet was worth twenty dollars. Did I need any cash that day or later in the week? Was it worth twenty dollars to hand to someone who is receiving money from everybody at that intersection and who would likely continue to receive more from the motorists who followed me? I paused, and then I chastised myself.

Paul tells the people of Corinth that God loves a cheerful giver, not one who feels compelled or out of a sense of obligation. Not only would this twenty-dollar gift help this woman, but it would help me remember that God has blessed me with everything that I have, including this remaining bill in my wallet. Furthermore, the inconvenience of the chore of heading back to the ATM to get more cash paled in comparison to the hardship that she would face in trying to find her next meal or a warm place to lay her head that night.

As I handed her the twenty-dollar bill, she thanked me. To reinforce the point that I had gotten to the right conclusion even despite my hesitation, she closed her eyes and raised her head to look upward to give thanks to God. While I scolded myself for not being a cheerful giver at the outset of our encounter (which lasted no more than 20 seconds), I thanked God for the opportunity to give something to this woman in her time of need. Although Paul later tells Timothy in his second letter "Guard the good treasure entrusted to you, with the help of the Holy Spirit living in us" (2 Timothy 1:14), he's not talking about guarding currency or property. He's talking about keeping the faith in Jesus Christ and spreading the Good News to those in need. We guard the good treasure by sharing some of our own.

BENEFITS OF GIVING

Just as authors in the generations before them, the people who wrote the letters in the New Testament focused on working and giving, as God's will. As a result, they also focused on the benefits of giving to the giver.

Paul led by example, and he encouraged early Christians to exhibit servant leadership: "Render service with enthusiasm, as to the Lord and not to men and women, knowing that whatever good we do, we will receive the same again from the Lord . . ." (Ephesians 6:7–8). Just as in the days of the Psalms, the early Christians learned that good works find favor with the Lord, "**Do not neglect to do good and to share what you have, for such sacrifices are pleasing to God**" (Hebrews 13:16, emphasis added).

Paul had a great way of describing the influence that early Christians had on each other and how they could grow the Church through sharing the Good News around the Mediterranean region: the sphere of action!

*We do not boast beyond limits, that is, in the labors of others; but our hope is that, as your faith increases, our **sphere of action** among you may be greatly enlarged, so that we may proclaim the [G]ood [N]ews in lands beyond you, without boasting of work already done in someone else's sphere of action. (2 Corinthians 10:15–16, emphasis added)*

The sphere of action is determined by each Christian, based on the gifts and abilities granted by God.

Paul told the early Christians in Rome that the sphere of action had to include generosity fueled by the Holy Spirit (see also Galatians 5:22). As a result, their giving to others would directly lead to gifts from God. "You will be enriched in every way for your great generosity, which will produce thanksgiving to God through us; for the rendering of this ministry not only supplies the needs of the saints but also overflows with many thanksgivings to God" (2 Corinthians 9:11–12; see also Romans 2:6–8).

John had another way of phrasing this notion by asking, "How does God's love abide in anyone who has the world's goods and sees a brother or sister in need and yet refuses help? Little children, **let us love, not in word or speech, but in truth and action**" (1 John 3:17–18, emphasis added). Two thousand years later, John's words ring true to the Christian Capitalist: to love your neighbor as yourself, put your money where your mouth is!

PAUL REDEFINES WEALTH

As we discussed in the first part of this book, the Torah and the Psalms developed a theme of riches being deceptive and having moral implications. Jesus likewise focused on the deceitfulness of riches and regularly taught His apostles and followers that it would be difficult for them to enter the Kingdom of Heaven if they focused on wealth. Instead, they needed to focus on a closer relationship with God and follow the path that He set out before them.

Paul and the other authors who wrote the letters to the early Christian churches built on these themes and took them one final step further: they redefined wealth! Instead of putting emphasis on Earthly possessions, Paul and the other authors of the letters to early Christians said the real riches come from following the way of Jesus Christ and the wisdom that comes with understanding God the way that Jesus taught.

While these messages included the usual warnings about the evil of riches, they likewise tried to teach early Christians that wealth was something that they had never seen before: **wealth was something that could be achieved by the poor without any material possessions at all!**

God's riches, wisdom, and knowledge surpass human understanding, but this wisdom and knowledge are available to believers through Jesus Christ: "O the depth of the riches and wisdom and knowledge of God! How unsearchable are [H]is judgments and how inscrutable [H]is ways!" (Romans 11:33). While God's wealth is unimaginable, people can gain riches through belief in Jesus Christ. Paul wrote to the early Church in Colossae:

> *I want their hearts to be encouraged and united in love, so that they may have all the riches of assured understanding and have the knowledge of God's mystery, that is,* **Christ [H]imself, in whom are hidden all the treasures of wisdom and knowledge.** *(Colossians 2:2–3, emphasis added)*

If wisdom and knowledge of Christ are the treasure, then even the poor can be rich!

Paul further uses an economic example to show that God's love is available to all through faith. "For what does the scripture say? 'Abraham believed God, and it was reckoned to him as righteousness.' Now to one who works, wages are not reckoned as a gift but as something due. But to one who without works trusts [H]im who justifies the ungodly, such faith is reckoned as righteousness" (Romans 4:3–5). Thus, the wages of faith are given by God to those who believe in Him through His only Son, Jesus Christ.

In Chapter 7 regarding early Christian views on work, we saw that James disagreed with Paul. James encouraged everyone to be "doers of the word" and argued that faith without good works to support it is meaningless. Nevertheless, as a business owner, manager, or worker, the Christian Capitalist understands that it's all about work **and** giving. If Paul was right and faith is all one needs to enter the Kingdom of Heaven, that is wonderful. The Christian Capitalist embraces the work, however, and appreciates that hard work leads to the ability to give more. If that is the path that James encourages everyone to follow, then that is wonderful, too!

Once he discusses the wages of faith, Paul further turns the notion of being rich around completely. He explains that riches come to everyone, even the poor, through Jesus Christ: **"For you know the generous act of our Lord Jesus Christ, that though [H]e was rich, yet for your sakes [H]e became poor, so that by [H]is poverty you might become rich"** (2 Corinthians 8:9, emphasis added). Furthermore, Paul tells the people of Ephesus:

> *Although I am the very least of all the saints, this grace was given to me to bring to the Gentiles the news of the boundless riches of Christ, and to make everyone see what is the plan of the mystery hidden for ages in God who created all things; so that through the Church the*

*wisdom of God in its rich variety might now be made
known to the rulers and authorities in the heavenly
places. (Ephesians 3:8–11)*

Thus, the riches of Christ come even to the poor, and that
benefit of boundless riches is available to all who believe in
God and follow the path of Jesus.

With the development of a theology focused on the
riches of belief in God through Jesus Christ, even for the
poor, it was only natural that Paul and the other authors of
the New Testament would then counsel folks to avoid the
deceitful nature of material possessions. The first notion was
that God provides everything, so people should not want
more: "For from [H]im and through [H]im and to [H]im
are all things . . ." (Romans 11:36).

Recalling Jesus's message about how God takes care of
the sparrows, the letter to the Hebrews likewise encourages
everyone to be content with what they have and not worry.
"**Keep your lives free from the love of money**, and be content
with what you have; for [H]e has said, 'I will never leave you
or forsake you.' So we can say with confidence, 'The Lord is
my helper; I will not be afraid. What can anyone do to me?'"
(Hebrews 13:5–6, emphasis added).

Finally, Paul puts the relationship between people and
material possessions squarely in God's hands: "Of course,
there is great gain in godliness combined with contentment;
for we brought nothing into the world, so that we can take
nothing out of it; but if we have food and clothing, we will be
content with these" (1 Timothy 6:6–8).

The next step after recognizing that God has provided
us with all things is to consider material possessions worthless. "More than that, I regard everything as loss because of
the surpassing value of knowing Christ Jesus my Lord. **For
[H]is sake I have suffered the loss of all things, and I regard**

them as rubbish, in order that I may gain Christ . . . I press on toward the goal for the prize of the heavenly call of God in Christ Jesus" (Philippians 3:8, 14, emphasis added).

John adopted this theme, too. He told the early Christians that not only would the love of material possessions interfere with a closer relationship with God, but that the key to eternal life with God was avoiding these things:

> *Do not love the world or the things in the world. The love of the Father is not in those who love the world; for all that is in the world—the desire of the flesh, the desire of the eyes, the pride in riches—comes not from the Father but from the world. And the world and its desire are passing away, but those who do the will of God live forever. (1 John 2:15–17)*

Both John and Paul foresee the fate of those unable to have this perspective about their worldly belongings; they will be deceived about these possessions. This notion is revealed when John accuses the people in the early Church in Laodicea in his prophecy: "'I know your works; you are neither cold nor hot. I wish that you were either cold or hot. because you are lukewarm, and neither cold nor hot, I am about to spit you out of my mouth.['] For you say, 'I am rich, I have prospered, and I need nothing.' You do not realize that you are wretched, pitiable, poor, blind, and naked" (Revelation 3:15–17). This notion of the rich actually being poor is part of the deceitfulness of riches about which Jesus warned His apostles and followers.

As a result, Paul and James help everyone draw the connection between money and evil based on this deception:

> *But those who want to be rich fall into temptation and are trapped by many senseless and harmful desires that plunge people into ruin and destruction. **For the***

*love of money is a root of all kinds of evil, and in
their eagerness to be rich some have wandered away
from the faith and pierced themselves with many pains.
(1 Timothy 6:9–10, emphasis added)*

James further admonished the early Christians:

*Let the believer who is lowly boast in being raised up,
and the rich in being brought low, because the rich will
disappear like a flower in the field. For the sun rises
with its scorching heat and withers the field; its flower
falls, and its beauty perishes. It is the same way with the
rich; in the midst of a busy life, they will wither away.
(James 1:9–11)*

In hearkening back to some of the themes in the Psalms, James
equates wealth and evil.

Unlike some of the Psalms, James leaves no room for
the rich who perform good works and provide for the poor
and needy. Just as in those earlier times, and like some of the
Psalms, James states that the rich must have gotten wealthy by
taking advantage of the poor. In encouraging the poor to be
strong in the face of adversity, he takes aim at the rich:

*Come now, you rich people, weep and wail for the mis-
eries that are coming to you. Your riches have rotted,
and your clothes are moth-eaten. Your gold and silver
have rusted, and their rust will be evidence against
you, and it will eat your flesh like fire. You have laid
up treasure for the last days. Listen! The wages of the
laborers who mowed your fields, which you kept back
by fraud, cry out, and the cries of the harvesters have
reached the ears of the Lord of hosts. You have lived on
the Earth in luxury and in pleasure; you have fattened*

your hearts in a day of slaughter. You have condemned
and murdered the righteous one, who does not resist
you. (James 5:1–6)

While James leaves no room for the rich who do the will of
God, the Christian Capitalist notes a couple of things about
James's theology. First, James was writing to an audience of
very poor early Christians, and they considered the riches of
the Romans and the ruling Jewish elite to be evil. For a popu-
list theologian like James, the rich made an easy target.

Second, and probably most important, James didn't ac-
knowledge the giving imperative that runs throughout the
Gospels. When he tells people to be "doers of the word," the
Christian Capitalist understands that this can include work, as
well as giving to the poor and needy. As Paul tells Timothy in
his first letter, by doing these good works, the rich store up for
themselves ". . . the treasure of a good foundation for the future,
so that they may take hold of the life that really is life" (1 Timothy 6:19). While money may be the root of all evil, the Christian Capitalist recognizes that money can also be the root of
good works and generous giving to others in the name of love.

COMMUNITY BUILT ON LOVE

Jesus told everyone that there were two great commandments.
First, we must love God above all else. Second, we must love
our neighbors as ourselves. Although Moses brought ten
commandments down from the mountain after speaking
with God, Jesus distilled them into these two. As a result,
early Christians tried in various ways to focus on the Second
Commandment when it came to building early churches and
Christian communities.

As we discussed in Chapter 7, Peter and the apostles in
Jerusalem experimented with communal living, which was
short-lived because of its lack of sustainability. Instead, most

early Christian leaders simply built churches into the existing social and economic frameworks of their communities. The added element, of course, was love—love through sharing, not out of compulsion, but simply from the joy and cheerfulness that comes from giving to someone else and putting that person's interest first. These communities built on love were not the utopian-style community that Peter envisioned, but they grew like wildfire around the ancient world and ultimately became the foundation for the global Church.

While Paul spent so much time and effort traveling around the Mediterranean region, planting churches, and working hard to spread the Good News to all, he tried to lead by example and show others that living in a community committed to the Gospel of Christ meant living in a community of love: "As you therefore have received Christ Jesus the Lord, continue to live your lives in [H]im" (Colossians 2:6). While Peter and the other apostles in Jerusalem interpreted living in the Gospel as a sort of communal living that ultimately was not sustainable, Paul helped build a community of love in every city or town that he visited.

Instead of trying to build a new type of community based on the Gospel, he brought the Gospel to every current community, regardless of type. "Therefore be imitators of God, as beloved children, and **live in love, as Christ loved us and gave [H]imself up for us**, a fragrant offering and sacrifice to God" (Ephesians 5:1–2, emphasis added; see also Philippians 1:27–30). The one common feature for each of these new churches that were being planted in communities around the Mediterranean region was love!

Paul tells the people of Colossae that they should live their lives through Jesus Christ, and

> *Above all, clothe yourselves with love, which binds everything together in perfect harmony. And let the peace*

of Christ rule in your hearts, to which indeed you were called in the one body. And be thankful. Let the word of Christ dwell in you richly; teach and admonish one another in all wisdom; and with gratitude in your hearts sing psalms, hymns, and spiritual songs to God. And whatever you do, in word or deed, do everything in the name of the Lord Jesus, giving thanks to God the Father through [H]im. (Colossians 3:14–17)

The Christian Capitalist recognizes that, just as love fuels generous giving, so does an attitude of gratitude!

In his letter to the early Christians in Ephesus, Paul connects the riches of God's glory to the giving heart that comes from following through Christ in the Holy Spirit. Once again, he recognizes that God is at work in those who believe in Him.

I pray that, according to the riches of [H]is glory, [H]e may grant that you may be strengthened in your inner being with power through [H]is Spirit, and that Christ may dwell in your hearts through faith, as you are being rooted and grounded in love. . . . Now to [H]im who by the power at work within us is able to accomplish abundantly far more than all we can ask or imagine, to [H]im be glory in the church and in Christ Jesus to all generations, forever and ever. Amen. (Ephesians 3:16–17, 20–21)

Through that power of love at work within believers from the Holy Spirit, Christian Capitalists can accomplish things that far surpass their expectations!

PART IV

THE CHRISTIAN
CAPITALIST

By the year 100 AD, most of the followers of Jesus during His ministry here on Earth were dead. As a result, in the second century and afterward, everyone who tried to follow the path set by Jesus was trying to interpret the Gospels and the letters from the apostolic fathers to the early Christian churches in ways that made them feel like they were doing God's will.

The final part of this book focuses on how people around the world have interpreted the teachings of Jesus regarding work and giving since He ascended into Heaven. It examines the early days of the Church, medieval times, and the Reformation views on the subject and concludes with a look at modern society and how work and giving are viewed today, primarily in the United States. The final chapter proposes ten principles of the Christian Capitalist Ethic in the hope that everyone will be encouraged to work hard and to give generously to the poor and needy in their communities.

CHAPTER 10

WORKING AND GIVING IN THE FIRST FIFTEEN HUNDRED YEARS OF CHRISTIANITY

As we discussed in Part III, Paul and the other apostolic fathers traveled all around the Mediterranean region, planting churches in existing communities. The location and nature of these communities were critical to the growth of Christianity. Both densely packed urban areas and remote rural areas provided fertile ground for new Christian communities.

Rodney Stark notes in his formative work, *The Rise of Christianity*, that Paul and the other early Christian missionaries were not visiting random cities throughout the Roman Empire. In fact, as Paul wrote in his letters, he was a Jew and blameless under the law of Israel. He was a pure persecutor of early Christians on behalf of the Jews before his miraculous conversion on the road to Damascus. Even the newly converted Paul fell into a completely expected itinerary of visiting synagogues around the Empire, however. In towns where he was not able to find a synagogue, he would preach the Good News at a temple built for the Roman gods.

As a result, the growth of the early Church can be attributed to a dual demographic dynamic: (1) Jews who were already separated from the temple culture in Jerusalem because they lived outside of Jerusalem and viewed Paul's teachings about Jesus as a reform movement; and (2) people who were looking for something more real than the garden variety of pagan gods at the time. While it is difficult to determine the percentage of Jewish and pagan converts in early Christianity, Stark does a thorough and comprehensive analysis of those early Christian communities and concludes that the growth of Christianity occurred primarily in cities around the Mediterranean region in those early days. This was a critical development for the early Church because Jesus's ministry in Galilee, Judea, and the surrounding areas was primarily rural in nature. As we have previously discussed, the majority of the examples that He uses in His parables fit an agricultural economy and audience familiar with it.

Much of the first-century growth of the Church was urban, however, and this in many ways is what led to its meteoric rise in the first two hundred years after Jesus's ascension. Using a sociological model, Stark calculates the early Christian population and arrives with a similar number to most other historians. With a growth rate of approximately 40 percent per decade, "the absolute number (as well as the percent Christian) [of the Roman Empire] suddenly shoots up between 250 and 300, just as historians have reported."[1]

While the traditional view of historians was that Emperor Constantine converted to Christianity and made Christianity the official religion of the Roman Empire because of his victory over the Visigoths at the Milvian Bridge in 312 AD, Stark takes a different angle: "So long as nothing changed in the conditions that sustained the 40-percent-a-decade growth rate, Constantine's conversion would be better seen as a response to the massive exponential wave in progress, not as its cause."[2]

Why is this important for a discussion of work and giving? Stark notes that the life of a typical person in first-century urban areas of the Mediterranean was particularly harsh. With very little infrastructure, constant lack of food and near complete lack of hygiene, urban areas of the Roman Empire were breeding grounds for disease and civil unrest. As a result, the Good News fell on ears that were hungry for it!

This was consistently true long before Constantine ruled Rome. In about 170 AD, Dionysius of Corinth wrote to the Roman Church: "[F]rom the start, it has been your custom to treat all Christians with unfailing kindness, and to send contributions to many churches in every city, sometimes alleviating the distress of those in need, sometimes providing for your brothers in the mines."[3] Dionysius confirms that the Christian tradition of giving to the poor and needy stretched outside of their communities and even to dangerous places like ancient Roman mines.

Stark dismisses preconceived notions of early Christians as primarily composed of lower-class, poor citizens. Instead, "Far from being a socially depressed group, then. . . . The Christians were dominated by a socially pretentious section of the population of big cities. Beyond that they seem to have drawn on a broad constituency, probably representing the household dependents of leading members."[4]

When times became particularly tough, furthermore, the Church provided a place for non-Christians to seek refuge in hospitality and for Christian converts to show their faith through good works. Stark provides a detailed analysis of two famines in particular that illustrates the point. "In 165 [AD], during the reign of Marcus Aurelius, a devastating epidemic [smallpox] swept through the Roman Empire. Then, in 251 [AD], a new and equally devastating epidemic [measles] again swept the Empire, hitting the rural areas as hard as the cities."[5]

During these plagues, the urban populations around the Mediterranean region were decimated by disease and death. Somehow, however, Christians survived and cared for those around them. Showing the mercies that Jesus instructed them about in the Gospel of Matthew, Christians helped their neighbors and loved them despite these catastrophic conditions. "Christianity revitalized life in Greco-Roman cities by providing new norms and new kinds of social relationships able to cope with many urgent urban problems. To cities filled with the homeless and impoverished, Christians offered charity as well as hope."[6]

Furthermore, Greco-Romans found Christianity much more meaningful and enriching than pagan worship because it focused on an emotion that had absolutely no place in pagan life: love.

"The simple phrase 'For God so loved the world . . .', would have puzzled an educated pagan. And the notion that the gods care how we treat one another would have been dismissed as patently absurd."[7] Love had no real place in an ancient philosophy: "classical philosophers regarded mercy and pity as pathological emotions—defects of character, to be avoided by all rational men. . . . Plato had removed the problem of beggars from his ideal state by dumping them over its borders."[8]

Thus, pagans flocked to Christianity because they yearned to feel loved by God and to love their neighbors.

The corollary that **because God loves humanity, Christians may not please God unless they love one another was something entirely new.** *Perhaps even more revolutionary was the principle that Christian*

love and charity must extend beyond the boundaries of
family and tribe, that it must extend to 'all those who
in every place call on the name of our Lord Jesus Christ'
[1 Corinthians 1:2]. Indeed, love and charity must ex-
tend beyond the Christian community.[9]

These tremendous social, philosophical, and religious developments created a complete shift in the ancient world. By
the middle of the fourth century, Christianity was no longer
practiced in the shadows or in the catacombs. It likewise wasn't
just a religion for the cities, notwithstanding Stark's detailed
analysis. It was also practiced in the most rural, harsh climates
on Earth.

EARLY MONASTIC COMMUNITIES WERE CENTERS OF INDUSTRY AND COMMERCE FOR THEIR COMMUNITIES

St. Pachomius and *Koinonia*

As we discussed earlier, *Koinonia* is the ancient Greek word
for a community of close-knit people. In particular, it implied
a brotherhood and a community built on love of neighbor.
Pachomius was a young pagan boy in Egypt who converted
to Christianity around 312 AD, just about the same time that
the Roman emperor, Constantine, converted to Christianity.
He is noteworthy, however, because, unlike the majority of
the Christians described by Rodney Stark, who lived in urban
areas around the Mediterranean region, Pachomius was part
of an equally important trend in the growth of early Christianity: communities in rural areas that were based on a set
of strict Christian rules or beliefs that set them apart from
other Christians.

While Peter and the early Christians in Jerusalem developed a community based on common beliefs, as we discussed

earlier in this book, that community eventually wound down because it wasn't sustainable. The early Christian monastic communities, however, took a much different approach. Instead of developing a community of believers that included men, women, and children from all social and demographic walks of life, the early monastic communities were based primarily on men who were willing to give up all their worldly possessions to live in a community based on prayer, reflection, work, and abstinence. This was certainly a new trend for Christians, and it exploded in popularity in the second century.

After serving the community near his hometown, Pachomius decided to move into the desert. This was a commitment to the ideals of prayer, poverty, and community service, which quickly led others to reach out to him to join his cause. Thus, while many monks in the desert during that time lived as hermits, Pachomius was known for having built communities of like-minded men in these rural areas off the Nile in Egypt. Even while they lived in the desert to help abstain from worldly pleasures and spent the bulk of their days praying, Pachomius and his brothers had to work to live. In the process, they also helped others live. Deeply rooted in their commitment to monastic life was a sense of love for their neighbor, and they worked so that they could give to other communities even as far as the religious center of ancient Christianity in Alexandria, Egypt.

Pachomius provided an early example to other monks and monastic communities. While he wasn't the first monk to live in the desert, he was a foundational figure for early Christianity in Egypt and created the model upon which other monastic communities later developed.

Even as a recent pagan convert, Pachomius showed early signs that he understood the basic concept of love of neighbor, or what would later be called charity after the Latin *caritas*.

In conformity with his original vow, the first three years of his Christian life were spent serving the surrounding villages in every possible way. Only after this apprenticeship to charity did he embrace the monastic life, and his entire career as a founder demonstrated his persistent ineradicable desire to give humble physical service as well as spiritual direction.[10]

Pachomius led as a servant to his brothers, and he built these monastic communities based on service to each other and the communities of people around them.

From all the evidence, this initial orientation to the service of humankind lay at the origin of the Koinonia, a society in which Pachomius united the brothers to serve them himself and to teach them to serve one another. Before Palamon the Anchorite, Pachomius had had another master whose unforgettable lesson provided the primary motivation for his entire work: the charity of the Christians of Thebes. Their generosity in helping strangers for the love of God became above all else the model for the Koinonia.[11]

The fact remains that Constantine and Pachomius had something to do with one another. Converted within a few months of each other, they worked interdependently, in both opposing and complementary ways. At the moment when Constantine, the first Christian emperor, was inaugurating a new era by opening the world to the Church and the Church to the world by making Christianity the official religion of the Roman Empire, Pachomius as the founder of *Koinonia* was establishing a Christian community withdrawn from the world.

Pachomius first started his community with a basic rule in 312 AD. In addition to reading and reciting Scripture, extensive prayer, and an extremely rugged lifestyle, Pachomius instructed the brothers in his community to work hard.

> *The rule of monastic life, according to what we have learned from those who went before us, is as follows: We always spend half the night, and often even from the evening to morning, in vigils and the recitation of the words of God, also doing manual work with threads, hairs, or palm-fibers, lest we be overcome by sleep. [We do this work] for our bodily subsistence also; and whatever is above, and beyond our needs we give to the poor, following the words of the Apostle [Paul],* **only let us remember the poor.**[12]

The Pachomian brothers took their charity outside the walls of the monastery and into the local village. "When he saw that a lot of people had come to live in the village, he took the brothers and went to build them a church where they could assemble. Besides, there were a lot of people all around that place. He took care of their offering because they were in a great state of poverty."[13]

Pachomius wasn't the only Christian leader to establish a monastic community in the desert in Egypt. In fact, he was part of a trend. Monasteries grew all over Egypt in the fourth century. In *The Lives of the Desert Fathers*, a group of dedicated Christians traveled around the Nile River Region in Egypt and found monasteries of all types and sizes. In their interviews with those monks and people in their communities, they gave modern readers a view into the way that those monastic communities were centers of agriculture and trade, as well as philanthropy, for the people around them.

Early Christians wanting to follow the way of Jesus flocked to the Egyptian desert along the Nile River. "While one of the themes for the monks themselves was a radical withdrawal from society and its concerns, they inevitably created a new focus of order. In a visible as well as a spiritual way, the monks made the desert blossom."[14] These monasteries soon became centers of industry and commerce for Alexandria, the largest city in Egypt and one of the centers of Christendom at that time.

How could these rural monasteries support the city? They had already taken care of the people in their surrounding communities! Sarapion, a monastic leader in the desert,

> *organized a regular trade between [the monastery] and the city of Alexandria on a large scale, sending wheat and clothing down to the poor of Alexandria; the reason given was that there were no poor near the monasteries: "From the labors of the brethren, they dispatch whole ship-loads of wheat and clothing to Alexandria for the poor, because it is rare for anyone in need to be found living near the monasteries."[15]*

These monks worked hard to create wheat fields and raise herds of livestock. "The work of the monk produces the fruits of charity and this is the concern of the monks, and of those who visited them."[16] In a continuation of the practice of the early churches of providing relief to others outside their community, Sarapion was able to manage a considerable relief effort.

> *Thanks to the labours of the community he successfully administered a considerable rural economy, for at harvest time all of them came as a body and brought him their own produce. . . . Through Sarapion, they provided this*

grain for the relief of the poor, so that there was nobody in that district who was destitute any longer. Indeed, wheat was even sent to the poor of Alexandria.[17]

The vow of poverty taken by these Egyptian monks was extreme. "Again, and again there were stories of converts who had wealth and either distributed it [to the poor] or took it with them into the desert."[18] In a foreshadowing of the medieval practice of collecting indulgences by the Church, one monk told the visitors that he gladly gave his wealth to the monastery in exchange for their prayers. "I have contributed my profit to the common fund, for I consider that this transaction, the sharing of what I have gained with the brethren, will be to my advantage, because then they will pray for my salvation."[19]

Notwithstanding the harsh climate of the desert, the monasteries were extremely popular, probably because of the unstable ancient urban life described by Rodney Stark. "The temples and capitals of the city [Oxyrhynchus, Egypt] were bursting with monks; every quarter of the city was inhabited by them. . . . In fact, there are said to be 5,000 monks within the walls and as many again outside and there is no hour of the day or night, when they do not offer a worship to God."[20] Even in the desert of Egypt, within 250 years of Jesus's ascension, Christian communities were thriving!

THE CHURCH LOSES ITS WAY IN THE MIDDLE AGES

By the early twelfth century, monasteries spread throughout Europe and became the centers of industry and commerce in their communities, including providing relief to the poor and needy. Fountains Abbey, in Yorkshire, England, is a good example. It "made a significant contribution to charity, distributing food, clothing, money and providing other support for the local poor."[21] In a sign of the medieval theology of choosing which poor people to assist in their communities based on the brothers' perception of the morality of the recipient, however, "charity did not extend to disreputable women or the lazy, for the monks were concerned to help the worthy and deserving poor."[22]

As a result, relief efforts were often reserved for the good times. "Accordingly, the administration of hospitality and charity was restricted at harvest time when work was plentiful and those in need could earn their bread."[23] Just as Paul told the early Christians, these monks had the attitude that if someone could work for their food, they should.

St. Francis and Mendicant Orders

Despite the noble Christian intentions of abbeys like the Fountains in Yorkshire, and the rules on which they were based, the Church at large and most abbeys began to waver from the initial core concepts embraced by the apostolic fathers. By the Middle Ages and early second millennia of Christianity, the rulers of the Church developed theology in an effort to preserve their power and kept both the rich and the poor members of their churches under their influence. Essentially, the Church's philosophy at the time was that God's grace was only extended to those who loved Him, and the best way to show that a person loved God was to provide some kind of material or financial benefit to the Church in exchange for a blessing.

These gifts in exchange for blessings, called indulgences, were used for centuries by Church leaders to fleece financial contributions from rich and poor alike around their communities. Ironically, this practice of collecting indulgences was not much different than the old Jewish practice that enraged Jesus in His time of temple officials selling doves and lambs for slaughter so that people could worship God.

Two men responded to this alarming trend in very different ways: Francis of Assisi and Thomas Aquinas.

Francis, who is usually associated in modern times with the love of animals and nature, was first and foremost an opponent of a monastic system that had developed into a perverse vehicle of wealth and privilege for monks throughout Europe. In response to these communities, which Francis believed were the opposite of what their vows purported them to be, he powered a trend of a new movement of mendicant monastic communities in the late thirteenth century.

These Mendicant orders were based on poverty, abstinence, and prayer to avoid the temptation of wealth and privilege that had corrupted so many of their predecessors. A Mendicant community took it one step further, however, by refraining from ownership of any material possessions at all, either on behalf of the individual monk or the monastic community itself. They traveled and begged without shame, preaching the Good News around Europe and the medieval world, primarily to the poor. Thus, the Mendicant monks depended on their audiences, including the poor, for their survival.

The *Rule of St. Francis* begins with these characteristic words: "The rule and life of the Minor Brothers is this, namely, to observe the holy Gospel of our Lord Jesus Christ by living in obedience, without property and in chastity."[24] Just as the *Rule of St. Benedict* six hundred years earlier (see Appendix B), the *Rule of St. Francis* goes into great detail regarding prayer, fasting, and other components of a humble life. "The forty days' fast . . . which begins Epiphany, is left free to the good will of the brothers. The brothers were to travel without shoes or ride on horseback, unless it was necessary, and under no circumstances were they to "receive coins or money."[25]

Like many of the preceding monastic communities, work was a key component of the life of a Franciscan monk. To banish idleness and to provide for their support, Francis insisted on the duty of working for "those brothers to whom the Lord has given the grace of working. But they must work in such a way that they do not extinguish the spirit of prayer and devotion, to which all temporal things must be subservient."[26]

The Rule of St. Francis provides insight into the kind of reform that Francis had in mind when disavowing the wealth and privilege of the existing monasteries of the time: "The brothers shall appropriate nothing to themselves, neither a house nor place nor anything. And as pilgrims and strangers in this world . . . let them go confidently in quest of alms."[27] Based on his plain reading of the Gospels, Francis determined that poverty was the key to the Kingdom of Heaven. "This, my dearest brothers, is the height of the most sublime poverty, which has made you heirs and kings of the [K]ingdom of [H]eaven: poor in goods, but exalted in virtue."[28]

Eventually, these mendicant orders flourished enough that the Church recognized and organized them. In 1274, the Second Council of Lyon established four main Mendicant orders, including the Franciscans and the Dominicans. These two orders would later send monks to the New World and set a new standard for hard work and generous giving.

These orders attempted to return to the early days of the apostles traveling around the Mediterranean region, bringing the Good News to those who hosted them, just as Jesus sent the original twelve apostles around Galilee. These people felt called by God just as if Jesus had sent them directly. "The choice to be poor was realized in a series of gestures: abandonment of one's paternal house, a wandering life, ragged appearance and clothes, manual work as scullery-man and mason, and begging without shame."[29]

St. Thomas Aquinas on Work and Giving

The other man to respond to this medieval crisis in theology and practice was Thomas Aquinas. Unlike Francis, who took to the road to express his desire to return to early Christian basics, Thomas Aquinas took an academic approach in the late thirteenth century that created the model for academic theology, and university life generally, that resounds today.

Aquinas held on to the theology developed by Peter, James, Paul, and other early Christian apostolic leaders. In his *Summa Theologiae*, he discussed the connection between God and man through work and giving. In fact, in foreshadowing the Christian Capitalist Ethic, Aquinas wrote that the main spiritual goal of work was to provide a benefit to others!

Aquinas provided four reasons that people perform manual labor. The first three relate to survival, combating idleness, and conquering evil. The fourth, however, is most important for spiritual purposes. He said that the fourth object of manual labor is almsgiving, the medieval phrase for giving to the poor and needy. **Thus, Aquinas contends that one of the key reasons that all humans work is to provide help to those in need.**[30]

To him, work and giving were so intertwined that he used the phrase **almsdeeds**, which combined works, which he would have also called **deeds**, and giving to the poor, which in his time was called almsgiving. In the *Summa Theologiae*, Aquinas writes extensively about the subject of **almsdeeds**. He placed charity, or love of neighbor, in such high esteem that it essentially served as the foundation for all virtues.[31]

As a result, Aquinas connects the love of neighbor and giving to the poor and needy. Love of neighbor, or charity, is the key to almsgiving. "Accordingly, almsgiving can be materially without charity, but to give alms formally (i.e. for God's sake) with the light and readiness, and all together as one ought, is not possible without charity."[32]

As both Jesus and Paul told their followers, Aquinas notes that riches can be deceitful and interfere with a person's relationship with God. While giving to the poor and needy benefits the recipient, it also benefits the giver. "Almsgiving belongs to liberality, and so far as liberality removes an obstacle to that act which might arise from excessive love of riches, the result of which is that one clings to them more than one ought."[33]

Finally, Aquinas showed the signs of medieval times in his discussion of almsdeeds by noting that giving should not be free and overly generous. He understood the limited resources available to help the poor and that those resources must be managed to provide the greatest impact to the community. "Thus we are warned to be careful in giving alms, and to give, not to one only, but to many, that we may profit many."[34] While Francis and Thomas Aquinas did what they could in the late Middle Ages to try and reform the Church through their actions and writings, the level of institutional bias and corruption was simply too great. What the Church needed was complete reform, and that process was to begin 250 years later.

CHAPTER 11

THE REFORMATION AND MODERN VIEWS ON WORKING AND GIVING

MARTIN LUTHER

Martin Luther was a monk who lived in Germany in the early 1500s. He saw the way that the Church leaders in Germany were abusing their parishioners with indulgences and other practices that struck him as inconsistent, even as heresy, compared to the teachings of Jesus and Paul. When he issued the Ninety-Five Theses in Wittenberg, Germany, on October 31, 1517, he sparked a fire that led to modern Christianity as we know it today.

While the Ninety-Five Theses addressed grievances that covered a number of different theological and practical concerns, Luther also had in mind a return to the basics of Christian life that were a fundamental part of the early Christian communities. The core of his belief was that love of God and love of neighbor had to be free from all the entanglements that the medieval Church had placed in the way of those relationships. As a result, he contended that icons (images of saints and other holy figures), monasteries, indulgences, and anything else that Luther thought might interfere with the relationship between God and humans should be completely banned. His reform agenda also focused heavily on the core concepts of work and giving.

While the bulk of Luther's theology was focused on people's faith, God's grace, and salvation, he regularly preached and wrote on the subjects of work and giving. Like his medieval predecessors, Luther knew that charitable good work was the key to showing love to neighbors. "**God does not need your good works, but your neighbor does**" is a modern quote attributed to Luther, who further emphasized that "good works do not make a man good, but a good man does good works."[1] Salvation did not come from works, it came from God. Nevertheless, Luther contended that people could display their faith through those works.

Based on his harsh critique of the Church, Luther likewise said that any kind of work met the definition of a good work, as long as the worker's heart was glorifying God through loving his or her neighbor. "Our expression 'vocational guidance' comes directly from Luther. God has called men to labor because he labors. He works at common occupations."[2] This calls on a concept discussed earlier in this book: humans work because God works, and people are created in God's image.

Love of neighbor is the key to a closer relationship with God. Luther's theory was that, if a person is to love their neighbor, and Christ loves all people, then a neighbor must be willing to sacrifice everything for their neighbor. In his biography *Here I Stand*, Roland Bainton summarizes Luther's position on this point succinctly. "This is the word which ought to be placarded as the epitome of Luther's ethic, that **a Christian must be a Christ to his neighbor**."[3] Likewise, people have to take care of their neighbors because they act as God wants them to when they do so. "God has no hands or feet of [H]is own. He must continue [H]is labors through human instruments. The lower the task, the better."[4]

In his short book from 1520, *On the Freedom of the Christian*, Luther elaborated on what it meant for a Christian to be a Christ to his or her neighbor.

> *In this we see clearly that the Apostle lays down this rule for a Christian life, that all our works should be directed to the advantage of others; since every Christian has such abundance through his faith, that all his other works and his whole life remain over and above, wherewith to serve and benefit his neighbor of spontaneous good will.*[5]

This may not have applied to all of Luther's neighbors, however. As was the case in medieval times, Luther tried to distinguish between the deserving poor and needy and those who were simply unwilling to work. Hearkening back to Paul, who famously took the position that those who do not work will not eat, Luther tried to separate those who were truly poor and needy from those who were simply, in his way of thinking, lazy. This had a direct impact on policy in his community. "The town counsel at Wittenberg issued the first city ordinance of the reformation. . . . Begging was forbidden. Those genuinely poor should be maintained from a common fund."[6]

One of the other significant topics that Luther addressed was wealth and its connection to hard work. He "became the champion of the pre-capitalist economy."[7] This was apparently unintentional, as he was a strong advocate for the poor in that feudal economy. Nevertheless, his advocacy of "abolition of monasticism and the expropriation of ecclesiastical goods [like icons], the branding of poverty as either a sin or at least a misfortune if not a disgrace, and the exaltation of work as the imitation of God stimulated distinctly the spirit of economic enterprise."[8] Indeed, Luther may not have been an advocate for pre-capitalism, but Bainton's description makes it sound like he would have loved Christian Capitalism!

JOHN WESLEY

Luther was obviously not the only theologian who led the Reformation. Among others, John Calvin, who led the Presbyterian movement, had similar sentiments on the relationship between God and humans regarding work and charity. These Reformation theologies were well settled two hundred years later when John Wesley began to develop his approach to reform theology.

Wesley was an Anglican priest who served in ministry in England until he moved to Savannah, Georgia, and became prominent in the development of the colonial Church in America. He found that even the Church of England was in need of reform just as its counterpart in Rome. Later called the Methodist tradition, Wesley and his followers focused on a return to the basics of early Christianity. This included a focus on work and giving.

In his Sermon Number 50, Wesley goes into great detail with his congregation about how they should work hard, generate wealth, and support the poor and needy in their communities.

> *"The love of money," we know, "is the root of all evil" but not the thing itself. The fault does not lie in the money, but in them that use it. It may be used ill; and what may not [b]ut it may likewise be used well: It is full as applicable to the best, as to the worst uses. It is*

> *of unspeakable service to all civilized nations, in all the common affairs of life: It is a most compendious instrument of transacting all manner of business, and (if we use it according to Christian wisdom) of doing all manner of good.*[9]

In order to be a faithful steward of the funds that God blesses each person to have, Wesley told the people in his congregation to follow three simple rules:

The first instruction Wesley gives to his congregation is to

> *[g]ain all you can.* .... *Gain all you can by honest industry. Use all possible diligence in your calling. Lose no time.* .... *If you understand yourself and your relation to God and man, you know you have none to spare.* .... *Every business will afford some employment sufficient for every day and every hour.* . . . *You have always something better to do, something that will profit you, more or less.*[10]

Once people have gained all that they can, the second rule of Christian prudence is "**Save all you can**. Do not throw the precious talent into the sea: Leave that folly to heathen philosophers. Do not throw it away in idle expenses, which is just the same as throwing it into the sea. Expend no part of it merely to gratify the desire of the flesh, the desire of the eye, or the pride of life."[11]

Having gained all that you can and then having saved all that you can, Wesley concludes with the third rule: **give all you can**. Just as Luther advised that people should be a Christ to their neighbors, Wesley connects the concept of work and giving together by reminding everyone that everything in creation belongs to God. All that people have is God's, and thus, they are stewards of it for only a brief time.

By giving to others, "all that is laid out in this manner is really given to God. You 'render unto God the things that are God's,' not only by what you give to the poor, but also by that which you expend in providing things needful for yourself and your household."[12]

By gaining all one can, saving all one can, and giving all one can, Wesley concludes that, ". . . in other words, give all you have to God."[13] Following these stewardship rules puts a person in a closer relationship with God.

> *But employ whatever God has trusted you with, in doing good, all possible good, in every possible kind and degree, to the household of faith, to all men! This is no small part of "the wisdom of the just." Give all ye have, as well as all ye are, a spiritual sacrifice to Him who withheld not from you [H]is Son, [H]is only Son: So "laying up in store for yourselves a good foundation against the time to come that ye may attain eternal life!"*[14]

Although Wesley preached this Sermon Number 50 over 250 years ago, it stands as a testament to the foundational principles of the Christian Capitalist. These themes will be echoed in the Christian Capitalist Ethic in the final chapter of this book.

GIVING AS PART OF THE AMERICAN WAY

When the Pilgrims arrived in Massachusetts from England in 1621, the entire expedition nearly failed due to disease and starvation. They celebrated the first Thanksgiving by giving God thanks for their survival and the cooperative spirit within their group of settlers, as well as the indigenous peoples who inhabited that area. Thus, from the first days, Americans of all religious paths have had a spirit of coming together to help those in need, especially when the going got tough.

Alexis de Tocqueville, the French author and political analyst, saw this immediately when he visited America a few decades after the French Revolution. He wanted to understand what made American democracy unique, and he ultimately determined that it is the people of the United States that make it different! He wrote:

> *Americans of all ages, all conditions, all minds constantly unite. Not only do they have commercial and industrial associations in which all take part, but they also have a thousand other kinds: religious, moral, grave, futile, very general and very particular, immense and very small; Americans use associations to give fêtes, to found seminaries, to build inns, to raise churches, to distribute books, to send missionaries to the antipodes; in this manner they create hospitals, prisons, schools. Finally, if it is a question of bringing to light a truth or developing a sentiment with the support of a great example, they associate.*
>
> *In America I encountered sorts of associations of which, I confess, I had no idea, and I often admired the infinite art with which the inhabitants of the United States managed to fix a common goal to the efforts of many men and to get them to advance to it freely.*[15]

Americans developed a private system of philanthropy during the eighteenth and nineteenth centuries that relied on a common interest in serving the community, especially the poor and needy.

The popularity of voluntary charitable organizations in the United States, even amid strengthening state and federal governments, suggests that perhaps these organizations, with their well-established structures and programs, were able to fill a gap in social welfare programs where the young government's efforts proved insufficient.[16]

The American approach to charity was based on grass-roots efforts by its people in a variety of ways, as a couple of examples show.

George Washington

Around the same time that these charitable organizations were being established and mendicant Spanish monks were establishing the missions in San Antonio, Texas (see Appendix B), George Washington was born in the colony of Virginia on February 22, 1732. While Washington was raised in a family in northern Virginia that made its living through agriculture, he learned the trade of surveying and worked steadily to perfect his craft as a young man.

When the French and Indian War broke out in 1754, he traded in his surveyor tools for a saber and became an officer in the Virginia militia, fighting on behalf of the King of England against the French and their Indian allies. Even in these early days as a military leader, he began to exercise the kind of servant leadership that led him to become recognized as the father of our country.

As the owner and operator of Mount Vernon, a sprawling farm in northern Virginia along the Potomac River, Washington began to develop his place in the community as a philanthropist and as a politician. Once he was elected to the Virginia legislature, it wasn't long before he became part of the Continental Congress. These two steps led to his legendary, most generous acts. In serving both as the Commander of the Continental Army and then later as the first president of the United States, Washington famously forsook any salary or compensation for his service. Instead, he wanted any amount that would be paid to him to support the two causes that defined his life and career: the Revolution and then later the infant federal government.

While his work at Mount Vernon in the army and as president is well documented and recognized by many Americans 230 years later, Washington's hard work and generosity to the poor and needy mark him as one of the first American Christian Capitalists.

Once he married Martha Custis, Washington truly came into his own as a Christian and in his business ventures. Ron Chernow, in his masterpiece biography called *Washington: A Life*, put particular emphasis on the marriage as reinforcement of the foundation for Washington's religious beliefs: "Her philosophic and religious outlook tallied well in most respects with George Washington's."[17] In turn, this had the effect of making generosity one of the hallmarks of their marriage. "That Washington believed in the need for good works as well as faith can be seen in his extensive charity. George and Martha Washington never turned away beggars at their doorstep."[18]

Before the Revolution, he was a leader in his congregation (Pohick Church in the Truro Parish of northern Virginia) and was elected to a board that governed a broad geographic area within the church's sphere of action. This action included building new churches and almsgiving to the poor and needy throughout that broad and diverse community.[19]

Washington took his religious duties as seriously as his military and political ones. He contributed a significant sum toward the construction of the altar and for the goldleaf for religious inscriptions at the church. In addition to serving on the board for more than twenty years, the board elected him its leader three times over those two decades. Even while leading the Continental Army against the British and winning the Revolutionary War, Washington maintained his role as a leader in the Church. With his daily devotionals and regular prayer both on the battlefield and at home, Washington was diligent in his personal spiritual habits. "Washington's pastor at Pohick Church before the war confirmed that he never knew so constant an attendant at church as Washington."[20]

Furthermore, due to the sprawling size of Mount Vernon, the Washingtons also worshiped at Christ Church in Alexandria. Washington was not only a member of Christ Church, but he also served on the board and bought a box pew for his family.[21]

After the Revolution, Washington continued his work in the Church, although it was very different from his earlier years. *The Washington Papers*, a set of Washington's letters, journals, and other documents, are compiled, maintained, and analyzed by individuals at the University of Virginia. They tell a good bit about Washington's opinions on hard work and generous giving based on his faith in God through His Son, Jesus Christ.

While he served as the Commander of the Continental Army, Washington directed his cousin and manager at Mount Vernon, Lund Washington, to continue to give generously to the poor and needy in northern Virginia. In November of 1775, he instructed Lund: "Let the [h]ospitality of the [h]ouse, with respect to the [p]oor, be kept up; Let no one go hungry away . . . and I have no objection to your giving my money in [c]harity to the amount of [f]orty or [f]ifty pounds a year, when you think it well bestowed. What I mean by having no objection, is that it is my desire that it should be done."[22]

Washington had a deep sense of obligation to give to the poor and needy in his community, regardless of where he served. The *Washington Papers* includes his personal ledgers and reflects his expenditures throughout his lifetime for charity. Even when serving as president, Washington regularly used his personal funds to provide support to the poor, even though he had refused compensation for his work on behalf of the new federal government! Furthermore, "Washington's secretary, Tobias Lear, recorded hundreds of individuals, churches, and other charities that, unbeknownst to the public, benefited from presidential largesse. Even leftovers from the executive mansion were transferred to a prison for needy inmates."[23]

Washington, like many of the other Founding Fathers, was a product of the Enlightenment. As a result, he did not regularly refer to Jesus Christ, instead making regular reference to "Providence" as it would guide his business, political, and philanthropic efforts. His many years of service as a member and on the board of two churches in Virginia clearly indicate that he was a leader of men but a follower of Jesus, despite some historians' arguments to the contrary.

An important window into Washington's soul regarding his hard work and generous giving as a Christian can be found in the letter that he wrote to his step-grandson, George Washington Parke Custis. While serving as president, Washington wrote him a series of letters that offered fatherly advice on subjects such as virtue, friendship, and charity. In one letter, Washington instructed Custis: "Never let an indigent person ask, without receiving something, if you have the means; always recollecting in what light the widow's mite was viewed."[24]

With his reference to the story of the widow's mite from the Gospels of Mark and Luke regarding generosity and the relative value of donations to the poor and needy, Washington provides a striking reflection that he felt was his duty to provide charity in the community. Washington believed that it is a person's duty to give to the poor and needy, no matter how much one has available to give.

THE PROSPERITY GOSPEL

While American theology in the nineteenth and early twentieth centuries focused on the prohibition of alcohol and the return to a virtuous life without sin, as well as two World Wars, it nonetheless continued to evolve. Christian theologians searched for new ways to relate to their congregations on the topics of work and giving. The resulting theology that developed, called the Prosperity Gospel, became popular in the postwar years and thrived at the end of the twentieth century.

Essentially, the Prosperity Gospel was based on a return to some of the basic concepts of the Psalms thousands of years earlier. If a person follows God's commandments, then that person will prosper financially. Many pastors who embraced the Prosperity Gospel offered a very similar concept: follow Jesus, and you'll get rich!

In the 1980s, wealth began to take on such importance in society that it became an end; as a result, any means to reach that end were justified for many people at that time. In the movie *Wall Street* in 1987, dealmaker and millionaire Gordon Gekko famously proclaimed that "greed works": this phrase became synonymous with the mentality of excess for many Americans in the 1980s. While Christian giving certainly wasn't dead, many Americans began to replace God with the idol of money and embrace the *Gospel of Wealth*, regardless of whether they had ever heard of Andrew Carnegie or his book by that name (see Appendix B). Christian theologians and pastors sought to make sense of this for their congregations, and the Prosperity Gospel began to gain popularity.

Unfortunately, the bulk of the giving that many of these pastors encouraged in the name of the Prosperity Gospel was to that pastor's church, not to the poor and needy. With the arrival of televangelists broadcasting to millions via satellite and featuring twenty-four-hour call centers to accept donations to their megachurches, some churches' practices of preying on their congregations with indulgences (blessings in exchange for cash) had come full circle. Despite four centuries of Reformation theology, many pastors in this era went right back to the unethical practices of medieval clergy: taking advantage of the members of their congregations for their own benefit by duping them into making financial contributions under the false pretense of a favorable relationship with God.

The Prosperity Gospel has led many Christians to become more devout believers, and certainly led them to work more, therefore generating more profit, but the main criticism of the Prosperity Gospel is that it focuses too much on self-benefit. This was not God's message in ancient times nor what Jesus taught His followers.

While many Christians embrace the Prosperity Gospel, prosperity without purpose is just a different form of greed. Instead, prosperity with the purpose of generating income or resources that will both benefit a person and those around them give meaning to that income. Without a fundamental commitment to giving, prosperity on its own leads to the development of wealth as a false idol, as Holy Scripture has warned people for thousands of years.

We believe what God has in mind for us, and what Jesus Christ teaches us, is to glorify God through hard work for the purpose of survival, sustainability, and even wealth, but these good works must be tied to a habit of generous giving to the poor and needy that increases as our prosperity increases. By sharing our material treasure with others, we lay for ourselves treasures in Heaven.

GIVING TODAY

Even as the Prosperity Gospel has thrived in the last couple of decades, so has the trend toward secular philanthropy. In fact, a new term has been coined only in the last fifteen years: *philanthrocapitalism*. This describes the philanthropic efforts of the wealthy to support the needy in their communities through the operation of charities as if they were businesses.[25] Likewise, federal tax policy guides many Americans in their giving. While charitable contributions have been income tax deductible for more than fifty years, the laws and rules regularly change.

Most recently, the tax reform law passed by Congress in 2017 changed the standard deduction, disincentivizing many Americans from giving for the pure reason of gaining that deduction. Although charitable giving across the United States dropped in the first year after the new law, it bounced back significantly during and immediately after the COVID-19 pandemic. In its most recent summary, Giving USA, a foundation that studies trends in charitable giving, reported that Americans gave a record $484.85 million in 2021,[26] a 4 percent increase over the new giving record set in 2020. Individuals gave the most, compared to other types of donors, and religious organizations received more donations than any other category.

After another festive Christmas, celebrating the birth of Jesus with our family of three kids who are now in college, my wife, Rebekah, remarked on how this was the first year that we heard the children talk about Christmas in terms of looking forward to giving gifts as opposed to receiving them. Without any prompting from us, each one of the kids mentioned to us separately that they were looking forward to giving a gift to their brother or sister and seeing their reaction. While some of the presents missed the mark with the recipient, Christmas revealed that our children had experienced more joy from giving than receiving, nonetheless. Why is this the case? Why is humankind equipped with this sentiment of joy in the first place? Furthermore, why do people find joy in giving?

Scientific studies have revealed that humans are not unique in experiencing happiness. Anyone who's ever observed a dog would describe a wagging tail from a treat, a game of fetch, or simply its owner arriving home from a long day as happiness in the dog. While humans experience happiness, too, joy is a different thing altogether. Joy is an overwhelming sense of pure happiness. Joy is a state of mind, while happiness is a temporary emotion.

The distinction between joy and happiness simply underscores the reason that we, as humans, have joy in the first place. We are made in God's image! What gives humans joy is based on the hardwiring in our DNA that God gave us in creation. While no one yet knows for sure how it works, God has created people to experience joy just as He does. It follows that He created us to experience joy in the manner that He does. The Christmas hymn, *Joy to the World*, expresses this beautifully. God loved us so much He gave us the gift of His son Jesus. Our reaction, as humans, was pure joy!

Nehemiah, the great builder from Hebrew Scripture, has a way of describing the connection between God and joy. He states that through a close relationship with God based on giving to those in need, we experience strength. "Then he said to them, 'Go your way, eat the fat and drink sweet wine **and send portions of them to those for whom nothing is prepared**, for this day is holy to our Lord; and do not be grieved, for the joy of the Lord is your strength'" (Nehemiah 8:10, emphasis added).

Dr. Laurie Santos is a psychology professor at Yale who has a popular podcast called *The Happiness Lab*. In a podcast episode from November 2022, Dr. Santos had a guest scientist, Dr. Lara Aknin from Simon Fraser University, who described social giving as a psychological phenomenon that leads to happiness among people who give money, as well as time, to their favorite charities. Her research showed that people who spent money on themselves, either in the form of routine, monthly spending, or in shopping for more special items, like a car or jewelry, had the same level of happiness. Those who gave money to charity, however, were consistently happier than the other group.[27] This consistent happiness is the basis for joy, so she literally found scientific support for the joy of giving!

While her scientific research is important because it establishes that giving to others makes people happy, it doesn't address the fundamental issue for our discussion, which is why people experience happiness from the act of giving to others. *Why* do humans have this chemical reaction in the first place? The answer, at least from the Christian Capitalist perspective, is that we are made in God's image to give, and giving to others causes us to experience joy. Joy is likewise a gift from God to His children.

Martin Luther, who spent a good bit of his time writing about why humans act the way they do in relationship to God, put his finger on it five hundred years ago. Luther echoed Thomas Aquinas by talking about the heart of the giver. Just as Paul said that the giver's heart is most important to God, and Aquinas told his followers and students that giving without love simply doesn't matter in the Kingdom of Heaven, Luther talked about how love defined a person and a person's relationship with God.

> *Here is the truly Christian life; here is faith really working by love; when a man applies himself with joy and love to the works of that freest servitude, in which he serves others voluntarily and for nought; himself abundantly satisfied in the fulness and riches of his own faith.*[28]

In a study on modern Christian giving, J. Clif Christopher concluded that modern Christians are sophisticated givers who no longer give simply because the offering plate is passed in front of them.

> *People want to make the world a better place to live. They want to believe that they can truly make a difference for the better. There is embedded in us, it seems,*

a desire to finish out our work on this Earth with a sense
that we amounted to something. To sum it up, people
*want to be a part of something that **changes lives.**[29]*

The Christian Capitalist understands that this dynamic results
from the dual nature of the longing all Christians have to give:
(1) we are made in God's image, and He created us to give;
and (2) the best way to follow Jesus's direction to love our
neighbors is to help give generously from the blessings that
God has given us and improve their lives.

CHAPTER 12

THE CHRISTIAN CAPITALIST ETHIC:

THE MORE WE MAKE, THE MORE WE GIVE!

Christianity in capitalist nations today finds itself at a theological crossroads. While some theologians claim that capitalism and Christianity are in stark opposition and always will be, some contend that Christianity is a path to wealth and that people should convert to a life following Christ so that they can prosper. Detractors of the Prosperity Gospel look more to socialist theory and find support in some of the verses from the Holy Scripture that are discussed in this book. Likewise, the philosophy of Karl Marx, in which everything is shared in common and distributed to people according to their needs, has a significant foothold around the world due to the continuing disparity between rich and poor. The ESG (ethical, social, governance) movement in capital markets is an indicator of this continuing trend to add moral principles to business conducted in capitalist economies.

The Christian Capitalist may understand and even embrace the Prosperity Gospel, and capitalism is the economic system in which that theology is most viable. If Christianity is to address and ultimately survive into the next thousand years, and capitalism is to peacefully coexist and even enhance the spread of the Good News around the world, the Prosperity Gospel must be put into the context of all Holy Scripture. While God promises wealth to those who follow Him, he also warns of its deceitfulness. While Jesus warns the rich that they cannot enter the Kingdom of Heaven without selling all their possessions, He likewise commands those who have wealth to help their neighbors.

Having reviewed thousands of years of human history and hundreds of verses from the Holy Scripture that refer to work, wealth, and giving, what do we make of all this?

Christians can work without giving, but they inherently know this is not God's will and that such purposeless work takes them off the path with Jesus.

Likewise, capitalists can be productive and make great fortunes, but without the purpose of generosity and love of neighbor, they can find themselves empty and drifting. Their work and the fortunes they amass are hollow if their only purpose is self-benefit.

The Christian Capitalist, therefore, embraces both the role of Christian and capitalist by working hard for the purpose of generating wealth and then giving to those in need in the name of Jesus Christ, thus bringing the Good News to all nations.

The Christian Capitalist Ethic is a set of principles upon which a person can attempt to follow the path to a closer relationship with God, as set out by Jesus Christ, through hard work and giving generously to the poor and needy.

The core principles of the Christian Capitalist Ethic include general principles that can be adapted to all industries, all types of businesses, and all types of personal involvement in those businesses. Because the Ethic serves as a mission statement to be adopted by Christian Capitalists who embrace these principles, it is phrased as a collective statement using "we."

In this way, the Ethic allows Christian Capitalists to articulate what compels us to follow the way of Jesus Christ by working hard to generate wealth and give more generously to people in our communities and around the world. This happens every day in every nation: the Christian Capitalist Ethic is simply a way to provide a theological basis for how and why people work so hard and give so generously in the hopes of supporting those who currently act in this manner and encouraging others to do so.

What follows, then, is a set of principles that a Christian Capitalist can embrace to provide some understanding of how work and giving are intertwined in God's plan for all humankind.

Principle 1. God created everything in the universe and on Earth. As a result, everything that we earn, make, or buy, including the currency involved in all those activities, is part of God's creation and a blessing from Him.

The first chapter of Genesis tells us that God created the universe, including everything on Earth. This story is eternal. Therefore, everything on Earth now, millions of years later, is still part of God's creation (Psalm 50:10). Make no mistake: private property is a critical component of capitalism. Christian Capitalists recognize that their personal property is ultimately a part of God's creation that they only possess for a brief time during their lives here on Earth.

Conservation and stewardship of God's creation both protect this property for future generations of that person's family and help the Christian Capitalist give more to others now.

When you have eaten your fill and have built fine houses and live in them, and when your herds and flocks have multiplied, and your silver and gold is multiplied, and all that you have is multiplied, then do not exalt yourself, forgetting the Lord your God, who brought you out of the land of Egypt, out of the house of slavery, who led you through the great and terrible wilderness, an arid wasteland with poisonous snakes and scorpions. He made water flow for you from flint rock, and fed you in the wilderness with manna that your ancestors did not know, to humble you and to test you, and in the end to do you good.

Do not say to yourself, "My power and the might of my own hands have produced this wealth for me." But remember the Lord your God, for it is [H]e who gives you power to get wealth, so that [H]e may confirm

[H]is covenant that he swore to your ancestors, as [H]e is doing today. (Deuteronomy 8:12–18)

As any entrepreneur knows, every business can be only a few steps from failure. The same is true with personal wealth. "The rich and the poor have this in common: the Lord is the maker of them all" (Proverbs 22:2).

King David summarizes this principle for Christian Capitalists three thousand years into the future, as he praises God for the blessings that He gave David:

> *Yours, O Lord, are the greatness, the power, the glory, the victory, and the majesty; for all that is in the heavens and on the Earth is yours; yours is the kingdom, O Lord, and you are exalted as head above all.*
>
> *Riches and honor come from you, and you rule over all. In your hand are power and might; and it is in your hand to make great and to give strength to all.*
>
> *And now, our God, we give thanks to you and praise your glorious name.*
>
> *But who am I, and what is my people, that we should be able to make this freewill offering? For all things come from you, and we have given only what comes from your hand. (1 Chronicles 29:11–14)*

When we give to others freely, we recognize that we are sharing the blessings that God has given us, and we do so in the name of Jesus Christ.

Principle 2. All humans are made in God's image. Because God worked to create the universe and Earth, He created us to work. Work creates an opportunity to open our hearts in spirit and truth to glorify God.

The first chapter of Genesis tells us that God worked for six days to create the universe and Earth, then He rested on the seventh (or sabbath) day. It also states: "Then God said: "Let us make humankind in our image . . ." (Genesis 1:26). The Christian Capitalist understands that, in any walk of life, he or she must work to provide for his or her individual needs, as well as his or her family. Work is a necessary part of life, gives people more full lives, and God created us to work.

Just as God worked hard to create the universe and Earth and led the people of Israel out of slavery in Egypt into freedom, we must likewise work hard. Every action God has taken or will ever take is perfect, and we must strive to be perfect as He is. "Be perfect, therefore, as your heavenly Father is perfect" (Matthew 5:48).

While we may never achieve perfection, we must strive to get there and work hard, as He does. Jesus likewise told His apostles and followers to perform good works, and this was echoed by James when he told everyone to be "doers of the word." As Paul tells the people of Thessalonica: "Finally, brothers and sisters, we ask and urge you in the Lord Jesus that, as you learned from us how you ought to live and to please God (as, in fact, you are doing), you should do so more and more" (1 Thessalonians 4:1). From work to earning to giving, we want more and more in the name of Jesus Christ!

Principle 3. Jesus came to the world to finish the work that God started. Now, we work hard in all walks of life to continue the work of Jesus. In all our work, we strive to go forth and make disciples of all nations, as Jesus instructed us in the Great Commission.

Jesus tells the disciples and followers that He was sent to Earth by God to do the will of God and complete His work (see John 4:34). After His death on the cross, and Resurrection, He likewise passed the torch to His Apostles and followers. In the Great Commission, Jesus instructs them to go forth and make disciples of all nations (see Matthew 28:19). This set of instructions applies to all Christians.

Christian Capitalists recognize that spiritual gifts vary from person to person. The Great Commission, therefore, compels the Christian Capitalist to bring the message of Christ to everyone regardless of the industry, business, or position they hold. Every walk of life provides an opportunity to shine the light of Christ to all through productive work and generous giving to the poor and needy. "And let people learn to devote themselves to good works in order to meet urgent needs, so that they may not be unproductive" (Titus 3:14).

The *Prayer of Saint Theresa of Avila* beautifully summarizes the reason that Christian Capitalists embrace this principle of hard work.

Christ has no body but yours,

No hands, no feet on Earth but yours,

Yours are the eyes with which He looks compassionately
    on this world,

Yours are the feet with which He walks to do good,

Yours are the hands, with which He blesses all the world.

Yours are the hands, yours are the feet,

Yours are the eyes, you are His body.

Christ has no body now but yours,

No hands, no feet on Earth but yours,

Yours are the eyes with which He looks compassionately
    on this world.

Christ has no body now on Earth but yours.

Principle 4. When work generates a benefit, whether it is material goods or currency, we should save as much as we can, to protect our interests and those of our families. Sound personal financial management includes investing to grow the funds that God has entrusted to us. The first step to loving our neighbors as ourselves is ensuring that we, and any family members who depend on us, are self-sufficient and do not become a burden to others. Solid personal financial responsibility is a key to accomplishing this goal.

> *This book of the law shall not depart out of your mouth; you shall meditate on it day and night, so that you may be careful to act in accordance with all that is written in it. For then you shall make your way prosperous, and then you shall be successful. I hereby command you: Be strong and courageous; do not be frightened or dismayed, for the Lord your God is with you wherever you go. (Joshua 1:8–9)*

A habit of saving is good personal stewardship of the resources entrusted to us by God. This includes saving for retirement or for education for our families. Likewise, diligence has its own reward: "The plans of the diligent lead surely to abundance, but everyone who is hasty comes only to want" (Proverbs 21:5). This diligence also extends to financial management: "Precious treasure remains in the house of the wise, but the fool devours it" (Proverbs 21:20). As John Wesley said, we must save all we can through responsible spending and consistently saving a portion of our income for emergencies, life needs, and retirement.

By investing in other business ventures, we share the blessings that God has given us with others. In this manner, investing and growing our own wealth puts us in a better financial position to give to others. The term Max Weber used to describe people engaged in new and different kinds of business, "heroic entrepreneurs," inspires us to act as heroic entrepreneurs for our neighbors in the name of Jesus Christ.

Principle 5. We cannot serve God and wealth, but we can serve God with our wealth. God loved us so much that He gave us His only son, Jesus, so that whoever believes in Him shall have eternal life. Because we are made in God's image, He likewise created us to give. In every walk of life, we must zealously pursue opportunities for financial gain so that we can share that wealth with others. The more we make, the more we give!

After our short- and long-term needs have been met, we should share the blessings that God has given us as a result of the work that we do with our neighbor. Whether the results of our work are goods or funds, we should invest those resources wisely to keep them growing and sustainable. As Jesus taught in His parables, God favors those who invest wisely and increase the blessings that God has given them. We should also plan for the future to ensure that we can care for ourselves and our families during our life here on Earth and for our families afterward. Once we've done that, we should plan to give generously from our estates. We should give frequently and generously to those in our community and around the world.

God's generosity in love extends to our salvation. He loved us all so much that he sent His only son so that whoever believes in Him will not perish but have eternal life (see John 3:16). This greatest gift, this ultimate sign of love and generosity, is a model for how we should live our lives and relate to others.

Jesus told us that we should love God above all else and love our neighbors as ourselves. The story of the Widow's Mite is particularly important to the Christian Capitalist. Jesus noted the generosity of the widow giving two coins to the poor because that was all she had, and it dwarfed the amount that the rich gave in comparison. Anyone can be a Christian Capitalist!

Although the tithing tradition began with Jacob in the Book of Genesis and was later written into the law of Moses, the Christian Capitalist recognizes that tithing is an ancient guideline and not a maximum to give to the poor and needy on an annual basis. Where possible, we will give more than ten percent and do so in a way that helps the poor and needy to release them from the bonds of poverty. We understand that giving a fish to a person will feed him or her for the day, but teaching the person to fish will feed him or her for a lifetime. "He who supplies seed to the sower and bread for food will supply and multiply your seed for sowing and increase the harvest of your righteousness" (2 Corinthians 9:10).

As an economic system, we recognize that capitalism is susceptible to abuse by those who are consumed by greed and pursue profit at all costs. We also recognize that capitalism is the system that has the potential to benefit everyone if those who accumulate wealth likewise love their neighbors and give generously to the poor and needy. The economic systems based on the philosophy of Karl Marx have failed consistently throughout human history, and those nations that initially adopted socialism have progressed in the direction of free enterprise.

Peter was with Jesus from the very first days of His ministry, however, and he heard every word our Lord preached and taught. The model of "to each according to his need" may not work as a government or community-enforced mandate, but we recognize that, after we have earned and saved all we can, we must give all we can to the poor and needy. Capitalism embraced by Christians provides a global basis for economic and personal freedom that allows every Christian to participate in the Great Commission: to go forth and make disciples of all nations.

Principle 6. Jesus taught us that we should love God above all else and love our neighbors as ourselves. We thank God for the blessings that He has given us by sharing them with the poor and needy in the name of Jesus Christ. He is the light of the world, and we shine that light to all.

Paul tells the early Christians in Corinth that even generous giving is nothing without love. In modern times, the following passage is frequently read at weddings, but it really has to do with relationships outside of family as much as it does marriage. "If I speak in the tongues of mortals and of angels, but do not have love, I am a noisy gong or a clanging cymbal. And if I have prophetic powers, and understand all mysteries and all knowledge, and if I have all faith, so as to remove mountains, but do not have love, I am nothing. **If I give away all my possessions, and if I hand over my body so that I may boast, but do not have love, I gain nothing**" (1 Corinthians 13:1–3, emphasis added). For the Christian Capitalist, however, this passage has a much different meaning. Without love for the recipient, the Christian Capitalist who gives to others doesn't accomplish the goal of following the path of Christ and entering the Kingdom of Heaven.

By giving generously to the poor and needy, we thank God by sharing the blessings that He has given us in the name of Jesus Christ, and we worship God in that process. This attitude of gratitude is critical for Christian Capitalists, regardless of how much wealth they accumulate. "Yes, everything is for your sake, so that grace, as it extends to more and more people, may increase thanksgiving, to the glory of God" (2 Corinthians 4:15).

Through gratitude and thanksgiving, God further strengthens us to do His work. As Paul told the Colossians, "May you be made strong with all the strength that comes from His glorious power, and may you be prepared to endure everything with patience, while joyfully giving thanks to the Father, who has enabled you to share in the inheritance of the saints in the light" (Colossians 1:11–12).

James likewise connects the concepts of good works and wisdom: "Show by your good life that your works are done with gentleness born of wisdom" (James 3:13). When "[w]hoever speaks must do so as one speaking the very words of God; whoever serves must do so with the strength that God supplies, so that God may be glorified in all things through Jesus Christ. To him belong the glory and the power forever and ever. Amen" (1 Peter 4:11).

Principle 7. We act as servant leaders in all business ventures, putting the interests of others first. Regardless of our role in the business, we lead by example and show others the path of Jesus.

"Guard the good treasure entrusted to you, with the help of the Holy Spirit living in us" (2 Timothy 1:14). When Paul wrote Timothy these words in his second letter, he wrote to him in Greek. "Good treasure" was originally παραθήκην (*parathēkēn*) which means a deposit or anything committed to one's charge or trust. Thus, the good treasure for Christian Capitalists has a dual meaning: we must guard the wealth that we accumulate in the name of the Lord to give to the poor and needy, and we must care for the light of Christ that has been entrusted to us through baptism.

We must be ready to sacrifice our interests for the good of others. Jesus explained this principle: "From everyone to whom much has been given, much will be required; and from the one to whom much has been entrusted, even more will be demanded" (Luke 12:48). As Martin Luther summarized fifteen hundred years later, the impact of the Golden Rule is clear:

> *I will therefore give myself, as a sort of Christ, to my neighbor,* as Christ has given Himself to me; and will do nothing in this life, except what I see will be needful, advantageous, and wholesome for my neighbor, since by faith I abound in all good things in Christ.[1]

When Jesus tells Peter and the apostles that it's easier for a camel to get through the eye of the needle than a rich man to get into heaven, they were all surprised. With his typical bluntness, Peter blurted out: "Who then will be saved?" Jesus reassures everyone that all they have sacrificed will be repaid a hundredfold and that they will inherit eternal life. Nevertheless, Jesus says: "But many who are first will be last, and the last will be first" (Matthew 19:30; see also Mark 10:31).

In 427 AD, Augustine of Hippo (in Egypt) delivered a sermon about love. In Greek, the word for God's unconditional love for people is *agape*; in Latin, it is *caritas*. In English, *caritas* became *charity*, and *charity* to this day is a word that reflects "love for one another."

> *Wherefore, brethren, cultivate charity, that sweet and efficacious bond of minds. Without it the rich man is poor, and with it the poor man is rich. . . . Cultivate it then, and, with it in your hearts, bring forth the fruits of justice. And whatever else, which I have not been able to express, you may find out for yourselves in praise of charity, let it be apparent in your lives.*[2]

In every job, from the first as a teenager until the last before retirement, we embrace the role of servant leader. As Christian Capitalists, we have much entrusted to us, and we take the light of Christ into every industry and every setting of work available in our capitalist economy. Regardless of the industry or type of job, we take our work ethic and attitude of gratitude into every setting presented by capitalism and shine the light of Christ before all.

Principle 8. When we give, we should give with humility. These gifts that we make to others are simply sharing the benefits that God has given us. While God loves a cheerful giver, he also loves a humble one.

We understand that we are mere stewards of God's creation. When we accumulate any material possessions, we act humbly because we have earned, grown, or built something that is a gift from God. Paul recognized this truth when he asked the people of Corinth: "What do you have that you did not receive? And if you received it, why do you boast as if it were not a gift?" (1 Corinthians 4:7). This is the way that Jesus instructed us to act: ". . . for all who exalt themselves will be humbled, but all who humble themselves will be exalted" (Luke 18:14).

While we may share our stories of giving with others to encourage and motivate them to do likewise, Jesus tells His apostles and followers that we should let God decide how to reward our efforts:

> So whenever you give alms, do not sound a trumpet before you, as the hypocrites do in the synagogues and in the streets, so that they may be praised by others. Truly I tell you, they have received their reward. But when you give alms, do not let your left hand know what your right hand is doing, so that your alms may be done in secret; and your Father who sees in secret will reward you. (Matthew 6:2–4)

Furthermore, when we give to the poor and needy by sharing God's creation with them to their benefit, we should not brag or boast. Instead, we should appreciate that it is our duty to give generously: "So you also, when you have done all that you were ordered to do, say, 'We are worthless slaves; we have done only what we ought to have done!'" (Luke 17:10).

Principle 9. True riches are based on wisdom and a closer relationship with God. Like the widow who gave two coins, we don't have to be wealthy to give to others. Likewise, we don't measure our wealth according to the amount of our material possessions. If we have wealth, however, we have to give generously.

When we thank God for His blessings by giving to others, we experience true joy. As Paul wrote in his first letter to Timothy, our attitude of gratitude carries direct benefits in the Kingdom of Heaven.

> *As for those who in the present age are rich, command them not to be haughty, or to set their hopes on the uncertainty of riches, but rather on God who richly provides us with everything for our enjoyment. **They are to do good, to be rich in good works, generous, and ready to share, thus storing up for themselves the treasure of a good foundation for the future, so that they may take hold of the life that really is life.*** (1 Timothy 6:17–19, emphasis added)*

Jesus regularly discusses the deceitfulness of riches with His apostles and followers. Calling upon the message of the Torah and the Psalms, He tells everyone that creating false idols with material wealth can interfere with a person's relationship with God. It doesn't have to do that, however.

Christian Capitalists understand that, by using our resources in the way that God wants us, we can accomplish His will. By serving others, we also secure a place in the Kingdom of Heaven. We thank God for the blessings of this life by sharing them with others.

> *Through the testing of this ministry you glorify God by your obedience to the confession of the [G]ospel of*

Christ and by the generosity of your sharing with them and with all others, while they long for you and pray for you because of the surpassing grace of God that [H]e has given you. Thanks be to God for [H]is indescribable gift! (2 Corinthians 9:13–15)

While Paul describes material possessions as rubbish to the people of Philippi, we understand that material possessions can be used to help others and spread the Good News. No minimum amount of giving is required to be a Christian Capitalist. Whether we have several million dollars in our 401(k) plan accounts, or we don't even know what a 401(k) is, we can act as Christian Capitalists using the widow giving her two coins as a role model. Some of the most generous Christians in history and today have been those that we would consider impoverished. Nevertheless, if someone only has two pennies, those are still a blessing from God to be shared with others!

Principle 10. The Gospel of Hard Work and Generous Giving recognizes that any material wealth we possess during our short time here on Earth is fleeting and temporary, just like our lives. The only true reward for working hard, accumulating wealth, and giving generously to others is joy in life and a place in the Kingdom of Heaven.

The way to get rich through the Gospel of Hard Work and Generous Giving is not just to accumulate wealth through free enterprise but to give generously from it. "You will be enriched in every way for your great generosity, which will produce thanksgiving to God through us; for the rendering of this ministry not only supplies the needs of the saints but also overflows with many thanksgivings to God" (2 Corinthians 9:11–12).

Jesus tells us to keep our hearts and minds focused on Heavenly things, and we do this even in our work and business. We know that Earthly things can interfere with our relationship with God: "And [H]e said to them, 'Take care! Be on your guard against all kinds of greed; for one's life does not consist in the abundance of possessions'" (Luke 12:15).

When we focus on a closer relationship with God, prosperity follows, however: "But strive first for the kingdom of God and [H]is righteousness, and all these things will be given to you as well" (Matthew 6:33). With that prosperity, we glorify God through our generosity to others and thereby give God reason to make room for us in the Kingdom of Heaven. "The point is this: the one who sows sparingly will also reap sparingly, and the one who sows bountifully will also reap bountifully" (2 Corinthians 9:6).

While the parable of the workers in the field (in which every worker earns the same amount, regardless of the time each worker spent in the field) makes no sense from an economic or human resources perspective, the Christian Capitalist realizes that the message is not about paying a fair hourly wage to a person for performing work. Instead, the parable is about the broadness of God's love and that it's never too late for people to make their paths straight. "Surely goodness and mercy shall follow me all the days of my life, and I shall dwell in the house of the Lord my whole life long" (Psalm 23:6).

When God blesses us with the ability to work hard, and we give generously to the poor and needy, we experience yet another gift from God: joy!

> *Likewise all to whom God gives wealth and possessions and whom he enables to enjoy them, and to accept their lot and find enjoyment in their toil—this is the gift of God. For they will scarcely brood over the days of their lives, because God keeps them occupied with the joy of their hearts. (Ecclesiastes 5:19–20)*

For people reading this book who have accumulated any kind of wealth, but now realize that they have never given anything to the poor and needy, this book is a clarion call to act now and support the people in their communities and around the world who cry out for help every day. A person may have a fancy house, luxury cars, and even a plane or a boat, but none of it matters without loving our neighbor and giving generously to those in need!

The path of Jesus through serving as a Christian Capitalist is open to all.

Appendix A

The Christian Capitalist Ethic

Principle 1. God created everything in the universe and on Earth. As a result, everything that we earn, make, or buy, including the currency involved in all those activities, is part of God's creation and a blessing from Him.

Principle 2. All humans are made in God's image. Because God worked to create the universe and Earth, He created us to work. Work creates an opportunity to open our hearts in spirit and truth to glorify God.

Principle 3. Jesus came to the world to finish the work that God started. Now, we work hard in all walks of life to continue the work of Jesus. In all our work, we strive to go forth and make disciples of all nations, as Jesus instructed us in the Great Commission.

Principle 4. When work generates a benefit, whether it is material goods or currency, we should save as much as we can, to protect our interests and those of our families. Sound personal financial management includes investing to grow the funds that God has entrusted to us.

Principle 5. We cannot serve God and wealth, but we can serve God with our wealth. God loved us so much that He gave us His only son, Jesus, so that whoever believes in Him shall have eternal life. Because we are made in God's image, He likewise created us to give. In every walk of life, we must zealously pursue opportunities for financial gain so that we can share that wealth with others. The more we make, the more we give!

Principle 6. Jesus taught us that we should love God above all else and love our neighbors as ourselves. We thank God for the blessings that He has given us by sharing them with the poor and needy in the name of Jesus Christ. He is the light of the world, and we shine that light to all.

Principle 7. We act as servant leaders in all business ventures, putting the interests of others first. Regardless of our role in the business, we lead by example and show others the path of Jesus.

Principle 8. When we give, we should give with humility. These gifts that we make to others are simply sharing the benefits that God has given us. While God loves a cheerful giver, he also loves a humble one.

Principle 9. True riches are based on wisdom and a closer relationship with God. Like the widow who gave two coins, we don't have to be wealthy to give to others. Likewise, we don't measure our wealth according to the amount of our material possessions. If we have wealth, however, we have to give generously.

Principle 10. The Gospel of Hard Work and Generous Giving recognizes that any material wealth we possess during our short time here on Earth is fleeting and temporary, just like our lives. The only true reward for working hard, accumulating wealth, and giving generously to others is joy in life and a place in the Kingdom of Heaven.

APPENDIX B

ADDITIONAL STORIES OF CHRISTIAN WORK AND GIVING

THE RULE OF ST. BASIL

While Pachomius developed *koinonia* or community living of these Christian brothers in the Egyptian desert, Basil of Caesarea, who lived around the time of Pachomius, followed along the same path. Historians wrote about Pachomius and his brothers, but Basil took careful steps to put his monastic philosophy in writing about 356 AD. "Poverty, obedience, renunciation, and self-abnegation are the virtues which St. Basil made the foundation of monastic life."[1] With these qualities memorialized, along with a commitment to all manner of works of charity, the *Rule of St. Basil* became the benchmark for Christian monastic communities in the eastern Orthodox regions of Christianity, and it still influences those communities today.

THE RULE OF ST. BENEDICT

Only a few centuries after Pachomius, Basil, and Augustine, one of the most famous monks of early Christian times developed his own community but after some life-threatening drama! Benedict of Nursia decided to follow the path of Christ by creating his own monastic community around 600 AD. After the dozen or so men he recruited tried to kill him because of his overly conservative and disciplined practices of prayer, abstinence, poverty, and hard work, Benedict created a new community based on the practices that he so tightly embraced. His second try at a monastic community in Italy stuck, and even today, Benedictine monks serve their communities around the world in accordance with the *Rule of St. Benedict*.

While prayer, abstinence, poverty, and hard work were at the core of Benedict's rule, love of neighbor became the foundation for the way the brothers related to each other and the communities that were around them. Like the monasteries of Pachomius and Basil, the monasteries established by Benedict flourished around Italy and later, all over Europe. They became centers of industry and commerce, where brothers would take on crafts or trades to make goods for their own use, and for those of the community. Meanwhile, these monasteries developed agricultural capabilities that created a model for secular communities throughout Europe. The agricultural and technological developments in these monasteries for the next thousand years are still in use today; from animal caretaking to brewing beer, these monastic communities were set to serve the poor and the needy in the communities around them.

The *Rule of St. Benedict*, which is typically published in modern times in a small booklet that makes it easy to read and use for meditation and reflection, prescribes many of the practices that the other religious orders embraced. Here, though,

Benedict instructs the members of the order directly on key issues that he had developed from his own experience. For starters, "the labor of obedience will bring you back to Him from whom you had drifted through the sloth of disobedience."[3] Discipline came first in Benedict's community of brothers.

With discipline, Benedict then gave instructions on many aspects of life in the order. "First of all, every time you begin a good work, you must pray to Him most earnestly to bring it to perfection."[4] As Paul told the early Church, the work is based on the blessings that God provides to all people. "With [H]is good gifts, which are in us, we must obey [H]im at all times."[5] With this recognition of the blessings from God, Benedict instructed his followers on getting to work and cited Paul. "Clothed then with faith and the performance of good works, let us set out on this way, with the Gospel for our guide, that we may deserve to see him *who has called us to his kingdom*" [1 Thessalonians 2:12].[6]

The work to be performed by the Benedictine monks was very focused. They had to work to build a community and survive. Then, Benedict told his order, "You must relieve the lot of the poor, clothe the naked, visit the sick [Matthew 25:36], and bury the dead. Go to help the troubled and console the sorrowing."[7] In this way, they could bring the Good News to the poor, and they would be known for their love. "Your way of acting should be different from the world's way, the love of Christ must come before all else."[8] This duty extended to those in the surrounding communities of the monastery that the monks visited, as well as those who visited the monastery. "Great care and concern are to be shown in receiving poor people and pilgrims, because in them more particularly Christ is received."[9]

These monastic centers of industry and commerce often led to the brothers developing trades or crafts that could be sold in the surrounding communities. Anticipating that this might lead to the development of wealth through the sale of these goods, Benedict tried to instill in the brothers a sense of giving to the poor, even when that entailed selling a good or object that they had developed at the monastery.

> *Whenever products of these artisans are sold, those responsible for the sale must not dare to practice any fraud. Let them always remember Ananias and Sapphira, who incurred bodily death [Acts 5:1–11], lest they and all who perpetrate the fraud in monastery affairs suffer spiritual death. The evil of avarice must have no part in establishing prices, which should, therefore, always be a little lower than people outside the monastery are able to set,* **so that in all things God may be glorified** *[1 Peter 4:11].*[10]

By recalling the sad tale of Ananais and Sapphira, Benedict also leveled a threat to the brothers of the order: **give everyone a good deal when you sell them something, or else!** Likewise, even in the year 600 AD, he advocated for a principle that later would become a staple of capitalism: as "not-for-profit" organizations, Benedictine monasteries should set competitive pricing for their goods compared to those produced in the surrounding communities by secular businesses.

While the *Rule of St. Benedict* required the brothers to work and serve the poor, it also required extreme poverty from the brothers. As was the case with the preceding monastic orders, Benedict required austere conditions: "no one may presume to give, receive or retain anything as his own, nothing at all—not a book, writing tablets or stylus—in short, not a single item. . . . All things should be the common possession of all, as it is written, so that no one presumes to call anything his own" [Acts 4:32].[11] This hearkening back to the days of the communal living of Peter and his followers in Jerusalem was intentional, as men joined the Benedictine order to be closer to the path that Jesus set before them.

This commitment to poverty even required action before a person took the vow. Brothers, or their families, had to put their vows and any donations to the monastery in writing. "If he has any possessions, he should either give them to the poor beforehand, or make a formal donation of them to the monastery, without keeping back a single thing for himself, well aware that from that day he will not have even his own body at his disposal."[12]

The *Rule of St. Benedict* is often summarized by the Latin motto *ora et labora* (pray and work), as that describes the commitments of all monks to the *opus dei*, Latin for the "work of God." While the monasteries established by Christians following the *Rule of St. Benedict* flourished throughout the Middle Ages, it was not long before the core concepts were forgotten by those who claimed to follow the *Rule of St. Benedict* but did not put those concepts into practice.

CHRISTIANITY ON THE AMERICAN FRONTIER: SAN ANTONIO MISSIONS

Four hundred years after they were established by the Second Council of Lyon, Franciscan and Dominican monks, as well as Jesuit missionaries to the New World, arrived with the explorers. Beginning in the mid-1600s, Mendicant Franciscan brothers came to the New World with the goal of spreading the Good News and building the Church in a completely new way. While still vowing poverty, abstinence, and a life of prayer, these monks also had a terrific sense of adventure, leaving Europe and thousand-year-old monasteries behind and heading out into the great unknown!

The San Antonio Missions provide an example of the kinds of communities that these monks built. In addition to traveling with settlers from Spain and arriving in the New World to build a community, these monks felt called to spread the Good News to the indigenous peoples of central Texas. The conquistadors were long gone, and the Spanish influence was still significant 150 years later. As they arrived in central Texas, the monks and the Spanish settlers worked with the indigenous people to build communities centered around a church. While teaching the local people how to modernize their agricultural practices and care for herds of domesticated animals, they likewise taught them about God.

In the process, these missions became communities centered around the church, but they ultimately sent the people who lived near them out into the broader region to develop communities on their own. Some modern scholars have criticized the mission system because of the deadly effects of the diseases that the monks and Spanish settlers unknowingly brought to the indigenous people living there, as well as the exploitative nature of colonialism generally. Nevertheless, the six core missions that followed the path of the San Antonio

River and were built between 1712 and 1730 became the center of a metropolitan area that today has over one million residents. The churches at these missions today have vibrant congregations. The oldest and most famous of the missions, of course, is Mission San Antonio de Valero, otherwise known as the Alamo.

While God brought the Franciscan monks, Spanish settlers, and indigenous peoples together, the focus of their gathering was to work. Not only did they work to build the churches, community facilities, and residences around them, but they also worked the fields, raised herds, fished in the river, and learned more about God and the path of Jesus.

The construction of these missions not only strengthened the existing foundation of trades, crafts, and businesses, but it also contributed to increased financial stability of the community. While some residents of the missions experienced financial success and growth, not everyone achieved the same level of prosperity. This disparity highlights a parallel between central Texas and European communities, as a core principle of the San Antonio missions was to care for the poor in those areas by sharing goods produced by the monks and other residents, just as their European predecessors had.

MAX WEBER AND THE PROTESTANT WORK ETHIC

The Industrial Revolution was creating a significant divide between rich and poor, and philosophers like Karl Marx and Friedrich Nietzsche analyzed this economy in new and sometimes revolutionary ways. One of their contemporaries, Max Weber, was a German economist and sociologist who wrote extensively about work and money. In particular, he contended that the Protestant Reformation played a crucial role in the development of capitalism. On the eve of the First World War and the Communist Revolution, Weber wrote *The Protestant Ethic and the Spirit of Capitalism* in a series of essays between 1904 and 1905.

As Weber concluded his essays, he likewise contended that the religious elements of the Protestant Work Ethic had faded from European society. Weber called on a Founding Father of America, Benjamin Franklin, to support some of his theories. Like Franklin, Weber emphasized frugality, hard work, progress, and thrift, but he held mostly secular arguments and did not focus on a scriptural source for their merit.

Like Luther, Weber noted that the definition of a "calling" had changed as a result of the Reformation. Along with the end of monasteries, the removal of icons from churches, and other movements against Catholicism, Luther and Weber agreed that a calling could now be used to describe anyone's vocation, as long as they worked in an effort to praise God. As a result, this de-emphasized religion in the life of the everyday worker, and that was supported by some of the secular theories on wealth adopted by Franklin. Nevertheless, during and immediately after the Reformation, the new Protestant religions compelled an individual to follow a secular vocation with as much zeal as possible.

Weber argued that the Protestant churches encouraged their members to refrain from using their hard-earned money on luxuries. Many Protestants no longer donated to their churches due to the rejection of icons and the end of indulgences. Furthermore, as Luther argued, Christians should not give money to the poor or to charity because it was seen as encouraging people to beg. Poverty was perceived as laziness, a burden to the community, and offensive to God. If a person didn't work, he failed to glorify God. The impact of this rejection of spending money in the Church, therefore, was the investment of this money into new business ventures. This provided an extreme boost to capitalism.

Without a tie to religion, therefore, Weber states that the spirit of capitalism is not a spirit in the religious sense, but an expression of ideas that embraced the rational pursuit of economic gain: "We shall nevertheless provisionally use the expression 'spirit of capitalism' for that attitude which, in the pursuit of a calling, strives systematically for profit for its own sake in the manner exemplified by Benjamin Franklin."[13]

Weber coins a new phrase to describe these secular workers who worked hard and earned money that they then invested in the new economy: **heroic entrepreneurs**.[14] To Weber, these heroic entrepreneurs would lead the world into a new economy with the spirit of capitalism. That was not necessarily a good development for mankind, however. In his conclusion to the book, Weber lamented that the loss of religious underpinning to capitalism's spirit has led to a kind of involuntary servitude to mechanized industry. One hundred twenty years later, man's reliance on artificial intelligence in business is consistent with Weber's concerns but would probably fall well beyond his imagination!

ANDREW CARNEGIE AND THE GOSPEL OF WEALTH

While Weber discussed the influence of Protestantism on the economy, a businessman and financial titan discussed the impact of the economy as a replacement for religion. Andrew Carnegie was a steel magnate in the late nineteenth century who made his fortune as the leader of US Steel. As the beneficiary of a monopoly like the other titans of industry of that day, he became wealthy in a manner that was really only comparable to a handful of other Americans. Carnegie understood the obligation of the wealthy to assist the poor, however, based on his upbringing as a Christian in Scotland; while he never spoke out against any Christian denomination, he wrote a book that took religion completely out of the relationship between the rich and the poor.

In the *Gospel of Wealth*, Carnegie contended that the wealthy are responsible for supporting the poor and needy in their communities. He wrote that the rich should "consider all surplus revenues which come to him simply as trust funds, which he is called upon to administer, and strictly bound as a matter of duty to administer in the manner which, in his judgment, is best calculated to produce the most beneficial results for the community."[15]

Furthermore, this support of the community should be sustainable, so it included components of both financial assistance and education as a means to prevent poverty in the future. Carnegie helped build libraries all over the nation in partnership with local governments to make them permanent fixtures of those communities.

The result of the *Gospel of Wealth*, which despite the name did not include the Good News that Jesus brought to the world nineteen hundred years earlier, was that Carnegie ultimately took a significant step in putting into action the theory that Weber developed. That is, the Protestant Work Ethic drove capitalism to the point that it looked to surpass religion and any obligations of the state to support the poor and needy in their communities. This philosophy is reflected in philanthrocapitalism today.

THE GIVING PLEDGE

A few Americans don't need charitable deductions to save on their tax bills. While philanthrocapitalism focuses on businesses giving to the community to make a positive social impact, the flip side of that coin is the Giving Pledge. Bill Gates, founder of Microsoft, developed this program in 2006 and invited wealthy people around the world to give away at least half of their financial resources. To date, 238 wealthy people have signed the Giving Pledge, including a number of famous US billionaires.[16] Those who accept the Giving Pledge recognize the obligation that the wealthy have to support the poor that Carnegie described a century earlier, but neither the philanthrocapitalism trend nor the Giving Pledge has any basis in love as their core principle. Jesus told us to love our neighbors as ourselves, and giving in His name should be based on love.

BIBLIOGRAPHY

Aquinas, Thomas. *Summa Theologiae.* Online ed. Edited by Kevin Knight, 2017. https://www.newadvent.org/summa/3187.htm.

Arnsberger, Paul, Melissa Ludlum, Margaret Riley, and Mark Stanton. "A History of the Tax-Exempt Sector: An SOI Perspective." *Statistics of Income Bulletin* (Winter 2008): 105–35.

Augustine. *Charity, The Hidden Meaning of Scripture.* Sermon 350, Opus Dei. Accessed August 27, 2023, https://opusdei.org/en/article/saint-augustine-on-charity-fulfilment-of-the-law/.

Bainton, Roland H. *Here I Stand: A Life of Martin Luther.* Nashville: Abingdon Press, 1950.

Bendix, Reinhard. *Max Weber: An Intellectual Portrait.* Berkeley: University of California Press, 1977.

Benedict. *The Rule of St. Benedict in English.* Edited by Timothy Fry. Collegeville, MN: The Liturgical Press, 1982.

Besse, J. "Rule of St. Basil." *The Catholic Encyclopedia.* New York: Robert Appleton Company, 1907. http://www.newadvent.org/cathen/02322a.htm.

Carnegie, Andrew. *"The Gospel of Wealth": The Nature of the Non-profit Sector.* Edited by J. Steven Ott. Boulder, CO: Westview Press, 2001.

Chernow, Ron. *Washington: A Life.* London: Penguin Press, 2010.

Christopher, J. Clif. *Not Your Parents' Offering Plate: A New Vision for Financial Stewardship.* Nashville: Abingdon Press, 2008.

"Churchwarden and Vestryman." *Mount Vernon.* George Washington Presidential Library. Accessed July 1, 2023, https://www.mountvernon.org/george-washington/religion/churchwarden-and-vestryman.

de Tocqueville, Alexis. *Democracy in America.* Edited by Harvey C. Mansfield and Delba Winthrop. Chicago: University of Chicago Press, 2000. https://press.uchicago.edu/Misc/Chicago/805328.html.

Francis. "Rule of Saint Francis." In *Catholic Encyclopedia*, edited by Charles Herbermann. New York: Robert Appleton Company, 1913. https://en.wikipedia.org/wiki/Catholic_Encyclopedia.

Garbooshian-Huggins, Adrina. "George Washington and Charity." *Washington Papers*, September 13, 2021. https://washingtonpapers.org/george-washington-and-charity/#:~:text=Washington%20practiced%20the%20advice%20he,in%20Philadelphia%20who%20needed%20help.

Griffin, Patrick. "Order of Servites." In *The Catholic Encyclopedia*, Vol. 13. New York: Robert Appleton Company, 1912.

Luther, Martin. *On the Freedom of the Christian.* In Henry Wace and C. A. Buccheim, *First Principles of the Reformation.* London: John Murray, 1883. Available from the *Internet Modern History Sourcebook*, Fordham University. https://sourcebooks.fordham.edu/mod/luther-freedomchristian.asp.

Nairn, Thomas. "'Begging Without Shame': Medieval Mendicant Orders Relied on Contributions." *Catholic Health Association of the United States: Health Progress.* March–April 2017. https://www.chausa.org/publications/health-progress/article/march-april-2017/%27begging-without-shame%27-medieval-mendicant-Orders-relied-on-contributions.

Pohick Episcopal Church. "A Historic Treasure." Lorton, VA: Pohick Episcopal Church, 2023. https://pohick.org /the-history-of-pohick-church/the-truro-parish-colonial -vestry-book/.

Russell, Norman. *The Lives of the Desert Fathers*. Kalamazoo, MI: Cistercian Publications, 1981.

Shea, Michael. "The Protestant Ethic and the Language of Austerity." *Discover Society*, no. 25 (October 6, 2015).

Stark, Rodney. *The Rise of Christianity*. Princeton, NJ: Harper-Collins, 1997.

Tsakiridis, George. "George Washington and Religion." *Mount Vernon*. George Washington Presidential Library. https://www .mountvernon.org/library/digitalhistory/digital-encyclopedia /article/george-washington-and-religion/.

Veilleux, Armand. *Pachomian Koinonia, Volume One: The Life of Saint Pachomius*. Kalamazoo, MI: Cistercian Publications, 1980.

Weber, Max. *The Protestant Ethic and the Spirit of Capitalism*. Edited by Peter Baehr and Gordon C. Wells. New York: Penguin Books, 2002.

Wesley, John. *Wesley's Sermon Reprints: The Use of Money*. Worcester, PA: Christian History Institute, 1982. https://christianhistory institute.org/magazine/article/wesleys-sermon-use-of-money.

ENDNOTES

INTRODUCTION

1. Statista Research Department, "Church Membership among Americans 2022," Statista, June 2, 2023, https://www.statista.com/statistics/245485/church-membership-among-americans/.

2. Pew Research Center, "Modest Declines in Positive Views of 'Socialism' and 'Capitalism' in U.S," September 19, 2022, https://www.pewresearch.org/politics/2022/09/19/modest-declines-in-positive-views-of-socialism-and-capitalism-in-u-s/.

3. Daniel Silliman, "Decline of Christianity Shows No Signs of Stopping," *Christianity Reporting*, September 13, 2022, https://www.christianitytoday.com/news/2022/september/christian-decline-inexorable-nones-rise-pew-study.html

CHAPTER 1

1. Unless otherwise noted, all Bible verses come from the New Revised Standard Version available at biblestudytools.com.

CHAPTER 7

1. Matthew Henry, "Acts 6," *Matthew Henry Commentary on the Whole Bible* (1710), available from *Bible Study Tools*, https://www.biblestudytools.com/commentaries/matthew-henry-complete/acts/6.html.

CHAPTER 10

1. Rodney Stark, *The Rise of Christianity* (Princeton, NJ: Harper-Collins, 1997), 8.

2. Stark, *Rise of Christianity*, 10.

3. Stark, *Rise of Christianity*, 9.

4. Stark, *Rise of Christianity*, 30.

5. Stark, *Rise of Christianity*, 73.

6. Stark, *Rise of Christianity*, 161.

7. Stark, *Rise of Christianity*, 211.

8. Stark, *Rise of Christianity*, 212.

9. Stark, *Rise of Christianity*, 212; emphasis added.

10. Armand Veilleux, ed., *Pachomian Koinonia, Volume One: The Life of Saint Pachomius* (Kalamazoo, MI: Cistercian Publications, Inc., 1980), xvii.

11. Veilleux, *Pachomian Koinonia*, xvii.

12. Veilleux, *Pachomian Koinonia*, 31; emphasis added.

13. Veilleux, *Pachomian Koinonia*, 47.

14. Norman Russell, ed., *The Lives of the Desert Fathers* (Kalamazoo, MI: Cistercian Publications, 1981), 13.

15. Russell, *Desert Fathers*, 13.

16. Russell, *Desert Fathers*, 45.

17. Russell, *Desert Fathers*, 102.

18. Russell, *Desert Fathers*, 14.

19. Russell, *Desert Fathers*, 49.

20. Russell, *Desert Fathers*, 67.

21. "Cistercian Charity," *Cistercians in Yorkshire Project*, https://www.dhi.ac.uk/cistercians/cistercian_life/monastic_life/charity/index.php.

22. "Cistercian Charity."

23. "Cistercian Charity."

24. Charles Herbermann, ed., "Rule of Saint Francis," in *The Catholic Encyclopedia* (New York: Robert Appleton Company, 1913), https://en.wikipedia.org/wiki/Catholic_Encyclopedia, c. iv.

25. Herbermann, "Rule of Saint Francis."

26. Herbermann, "Rule of Saint Francis," c. v.

27. Herbermann, "Rule of Saint Francis," c. v.

28. Herbermann, "Rule of Saint Francis," c. v.

29. Thomas Nairn, "'Begging Without Shame': Medieval Mendicant Orders Relied on Contributions," *Catholic Health Association of the United States: Health Progress,* March–April 2017, https://www.chausa.org/publications/health-progress/article/march-april-2017/%27begging-without-shame%27-medieval-mendicant-orders-relied-on-contributions.

30. St. Thomas Aquinas, *Summa Theologiae*, Question #187, Things That Are Competent to Religious, II–II q.187 a.3, available at *New Advent*, https://www.newadvent.org/summa/3187.htm.

31. St. Thomas Aquinas, *Summa Theologiae*, Question #32, Almsdeeds, II–II q.32 a.3, available at *New Advent*, https://www.newadvent.org/summa/3032.htm.

32. Aquinas, II–II q.32 a.1.

33. Aquinas,

34. Aquinas, II–II q.32 a.10.

CHAPTER 11

1. Roland H. Bainton, *Here I Stand: A Life of Martin Luther* (Nashville: Abingdon Press, 1950), 178; emphasis added.

2. Bainton, *Here I Stand*, 181.

3. Bainton, *Here I Stand*, 179; emphasis added.

4. Bainton, *Here I Stand*, 181.

5. Martin Luther, *On the Freedom of the Christian*, from Henry Wace and C. A. Buccheim, *First Principles of the Reformation* (London: John Murray, 1883) available from the *Internet Modern History Sourcebook*Fordham University, https://sourcebooks.fordham .edu/mod/luther-freedomchristian.asp, sec. 126.

6. Bainton, *Here I Stand*, 160.

7. Bainton, *Here I Stand*, 184.

8. Bainton, *Here I Stand*, 184.

9. John Wesley, *Wesley's Sermon Reprints: The Use of Money* (Worcester, PA: Christian History Institute, 1982), https://christianhistory institute.org/magazine/article/wesleys-sermon-use-of-money.

10. Wesley, *Wesley's Sermon Reprints*, part I, sec. 7; emphasis added.

11. Wesley, *Wesley's Sermon Reprints*, part II, sec. 1; emphasis added.

12. Wesley, *Wesley's Sermon Reprints*, part III, sec. 3.

13. Wesley, *Wesley's Sermon Reprints*, part III, sec. 3.

14. Wesley, *Wesley's Sermon Reprints*, part III, sec. 3.

15. Alexis de Tocqueville, *Democracy in America*, ed. Harvey C. Mansfield and Delba Winthrop (Chicago: University of Chicago Press, 2000), 489–92, https://press.uchicago.edu/Misc /Chicago/805328.html.

16. Paul Arnsberger, Melissa Ludlum, Margaret Riley, and Mark Stanton, "A History of the Tax-Exempt Sector: An SOI Perspective," *Statistics of Income Bulletin* (Winter 2008), 105.

17. Ron Chernow, *Washington: A Life* (London: Penguin Press, 2010), 82.

18. Chernow, *Washington*, 133.

19. Pohick Episcopal Church, "A Historic Treasure" (Lorton, VA: Pohick Episcopal Church, 2023), https://pohick.org /the-history-of-pohick-church/the-truro-parish-colonial-vestry-book/.

20. Pohick Episcopal Church, "A Historic Treasure," 132.

21. Pohick Episcopal Church, "A Historic Treasure," 130.

22. Adrina Garbooshian-Huggins, "George Washington and Charity," *Washington Papers*, September 13, 2021, https://washingtonpapers.org/george-washington-and-charity/#:~:text=Washington%20practiced%20the%20advice%20he,in%20Philadelphia%20who%20needed%20help.

23. Chernow, *Washington*, 133.

24. Garbooshian-Huggins, "George Washington and Charity."

25. Matthew Bishop and Michael Green, *Philanthrocapitalism: How the Rich Can Save the World* (New York: Bloomsbury Press, 2008).

26. Giving USA, "Where Did the Generosity Come From?" infographic, June 2022, https://givingusa.org/wp-content/uploads/2022/06/GivingUSA2022_Infographic.pdf.

27. Laurie Santos, "Giving Tuesday: Why Giving Money to Others Makes Us Happier," *The Happiness Lab with Dr. Laurie Santos*, November 28, 2022. This podcast can be found at https://www.pushkin.fm/podcasts/the-happiness-lab-with-dr-laurie-santos#episodes.

28. Luther, *On the Freedom of the Christian*.

29. J. Clif Christopher, *Not Your Parents' Offering Plate: A New Vision for Financial Stewardship* (Nashville: Abingdon Press, 2008), 13; emphasis added.

CHAPTER 12

1. Martin Luther, *On the Freedom of the Christian*, from Henry Wace and C. A. Buccheim, *First Principles of the Reformation* (London: John Murray, 1883), avilable from the *Internet Modern History Sourcebook*, Fordham University, https://sourcebooks.fordham.edu/mod/luther-freedomchristian.asp; emphasis added.

APPENDIX B

1. Jean Besse, "Rule of St. Basil," in *The Catholic Encyclopedia* (New York: Robert Appleton Company, 1907), accessed February 16, 2023, from New Advent: http://www.newadvent.org/cathen/02322a.htm.

2. St. Augustine, *Charity, The Hidden Meaning of Scripture*, Sermon 350, 2–3, *Opus Dei*, August 27, 2020, https://opusdei.org/en/article/saint-augustine-on-charity-fulfilment-of-the-law/.

3. Timothy Fry, ed., *The Rule of St. Benedict in English* (Collegeville, MN: The Liturgical Press, 1982), 15.

4. Fry, *Rule of St. Benedict*, 15.

5. Fry, *Rule of St. Benedict*, 15.

6. Fry, *Rule of St. Benedict*, 16.

7. Fry, *Rule of St. Benedict*, 27.

8. Fry, *Rule of St. Benedict*, 27.

9. Fry, *Rule of St. Benedict*, 74.

10. Fry, *Rule of St. Benedict*, 78.

11. Fry, *Rule of St. Benedict*, 56.

12. Fry, *Rule of St. Benedict*, 80.

13. Max Weber, *The Protestant Ethic and The Spirit of Capitalism*, ed. Peter Baehr and Gordon C. Wells (New York: Penguin Books, 2002), 19.

14. Reinhard Bendix, *Max Weber: An Intellectual Portrait* (Berkeley: University of California Press, 1977), 54–55.

15. Arnsberger et. al., "Tax-Exempt Sector," 105.

16. The Giving Pledge, "Frequently Asked Questions," https://givingpledge.org/faq.

BIBLICAL VERSE INDEX